Excel 2019 Beginner

EXCEL ESSENTIALS 2019 BOOK 1

M.L. HUMPHREY

CONTENTS

Introduction

Microsoft Excel is an amazing program and I am so grateful to have learned it because I use it all the time as a small business owner as well as personally.

It allows me to organize and track key information in a quick and easy manner and to automate a lot of the calculations I need.

For example, on a personal level I have a budget worksheet that lets me track whether my bills have been paid, how much I need to keep in my bank account, and where I am financially.

In my professional career I've used it in a number of ways, from analyzing a series of financial transactions to see if a customer was overcharged to performing a text-based comparison of regulatory requirements across multiple jurisdictions.

(While Excel works best for numerical purposes, it is often a good choice for text-based analysis as well, especially if you want to be able to sort your results or filter out and isolate certain results.)

The purpose of this specific guide is to teach you the basics of what you need to know to use Microsoft Excel on a daily basis. By the time you're done with this book you should be able to do over 95% of what you need to do in Microsoft Excel and should have a solid enough grounding in how Excel works and the additional help resources available that you can learn the rest.

The series does continue with *Excel 2019 Intermediate*, which covers more advanced topics such as pivot tables, charts, and conditional formatting, and *Excel 2019 Formulas & Functions*, which goes into more detail about how formulas and functions work in Excel and then discusses about a hundred of those functions, sixty in detail.

You are welcome to continue with those books but you shouldn't have to in order to work in Excel on a daily basis. This book should be enough for that.

It was written specifically for Excel 2019, so all of the screenshots in this book are from Excel 2019 which, as of the date I'm writing this, is the most recent version of Excel.

However, because this book is about the basics of Excel, even if you are working in a different version of Excel most of what we'll cover here should be the same. The basic functions of Excel (like copy, paste, save, etc.) haven't changed much in the twenty-five-plus years I've been using the program.

If you previously purchased *Excel for Beginners* which was written using Excel 2013, most of the content of this book is the same and you probably don't need to buy this book as well.

The visual appearance of Excel 2019 has been changed just enough from the 2013 version to be annoying, so it may help to have the updated screenshots, but don't feel that you need to buy this book to use Excel 2019 if you've already read *Excel for Beginners*.

This book is not a comprehensive guide to Excel. The goal here is to give you a solid grounding in Excel that will let you get started using it without bogging down in a lot of information you don't need when you're getting started.

In this book I will often cover multiple ways of doing the same thing to show you the various options available to you. I may not cover *all* of the possible ways of doing something (I think we're up to five or six ways of doing the same thing on some of this stuff), but I will usually cover at least two ways.

I highly recommend learning any of the control shortcuts that I give you. For example, to copy something you can use the Control key and the C key (which I will write as Ctrl + C). The reason to learn these shortcuts is because they have not changed in all the years I've been using Excel. Which means that even when Microsoft issues the next version of Excel and moves things around a bit (which they will because that's one major way they make money is through new product releases) you'll still know at least one easy way to perform the core tasks.

Also, when in doubt go with the right-click and open a dialogue version of doing something because that too seems to have remained relatively stable over the years and versions of Excel.

If what I just said didn't make sense to you, don't worry. The first thing we're going to do is cover basic terminology so that you know what I'm talking about when I say things.

Alright then. Let's get started with that.

Basic Terminology

First things first, we need to establish some basic terminology so that you know what I'm talking about when I refer to a cell or a row or a column, etc.

Column

Excel uses columns and rows to display information. Columns run across the top of the worksheet and, unless you've done something funky with your settings, are identified using letters of the alphabet. As you can see below, they start with A on the far left side and march right on through the alphabet (A, B, C, D, E, etc.).

If you scroll far enough to the right, you'll see that they continue on to a double alphabet (AA, AB, AC, etc.).

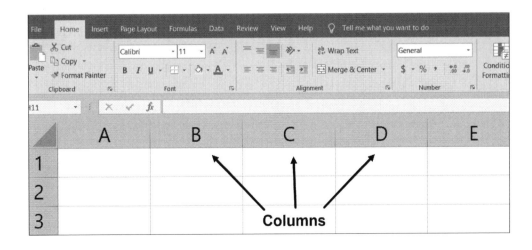

Columns

Row

Rows run down the side of the worksheet and are numbered starting at 1 and up to 1,048,576 in Excel 2019.

(Be aware that earlier versions of Excel have less rows in a worksheet so that if you have a lot of data that uses all of the available rows your file may not be compatible with earlier versions of Excel.)

You can click into any cell in a blank worksheet, hold down the ctrl key, and hit the down arrow to see just how many rows your version of Excel has. To return to the first row use the ctrl key and the up arrow.

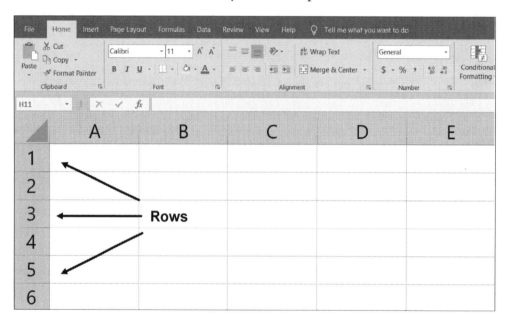

Cell

A cell is a combination of a column and row that is identified by the letter of the column it's in and the number of the row it's in.

For example, Cell A1 is the cell in the first column and the first row of the worksheet. When you've clicked on a specific cell it will have a darker border around the edges like in the image below.

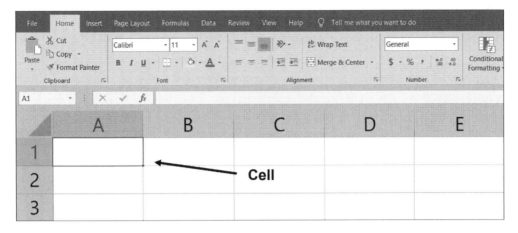

Cell

Click

If I tell you to click on something, that means to use your mouse (or trackpad) to move the arrow on the screen over to a specific location and left-click or right-click on the option. (See the next definition for the difference between left-click and right-click).

If you left-click, this selects the item. If you right-click, this generally creates a dropdown list of options to choose from.

If I don't tell you which to do, left- or right-click, then left-click.

Left-click/Right-click

If you look at your mouse or your trackpad, you generally have two flat buttons to press. One is on the left side, one is on the right. If I say left-click that means to press down on the button on the left. If I say right-click that means press down on the button on the right.

(If you're used to using Word you may already do this without even thinking about it. So, if that's the case then think of left-click as what you usually use to select text and right-click as what you use to see a menu of choices.)

Not all track pads have the left- and right-hand buttons. In that case, you'll basically want to press on either the bottom left-hand side of the track pad or the bottom right-hand side of the trackpad.

Spreadsheet

I'll try to avoid using this term, but if I do use it, I'll mean your entire Excel file. It's a little confusing because it can sometimes also be used to mean a specific worksheet, which is why I'll try to avoid it as much as possible.

Worksheet

A worksheet is basically a combination of rows and columns that you can enter data in. When you open an Excel file, it opens to worksheet one.

Excel 2019 has one worksheet available by default when a new file is opened and that worksheet is originally labeled Sheet1.

It is possible to add more worksheets to a workbook (that's the entire Excel file) and we will cover that later. When there are multiple worksheets, the name of the current worksheet is highlighted in white to show that it's in use.

Formula Bar

The formula bar is the long white bar at the top of the screen with the $f\chi$ symbol next to it.

If you click in a cell and start typing, you'll see that what you type appears not only in that cell, but in the formula bar as well. When you input a formula into a cell and then hit enter, the value returned by the formula will be what displays in the cell, but the formula will appear in the formula bar when you have that cell highlighted.

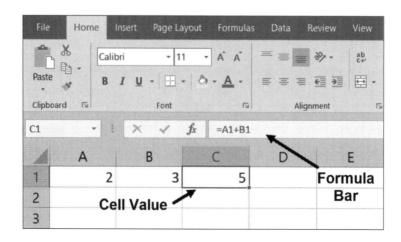

Tab

I refer to the menu choices at the top of the screen (File, Home, Insert, Page Layout, Formulas, Data, Review, View, and Help) as tabs. Note how they look like folder tabs from an old-time filing system when selected? That's why.

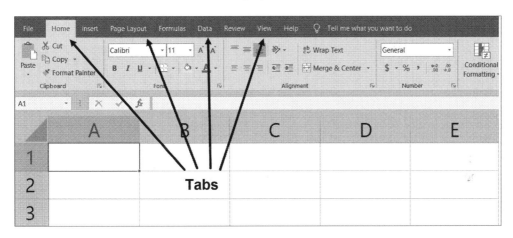

Each menu tab you select will show you different options. On my Home tab I can do things like copy/cut/paste, format cells, edit cells, and insert/delete cells, for example.

Scroll Bar

On the right side and along the bottom of the screen are two bars with arrows at the ends. If you left-click and hold on either bar you can move it back and forth between those arrows. This lets you see information that's off the page in your current view but part of the worksheet you're viewing.

You can also use the arrows at the ends of the scroll bar to do the same thing. Left-click on the arrow once to move it one line or column or left-click and hold to get it to move as far as it can go.

If you want to cover more rows/columns at a time you can click into the blank space on either side of the scroll bar to move an entire screen at a time, assuming you have enough data entered for that.

Using the scroll bars only lets you move to the end of the information you've already entered. You can use the arrows instead of clicking on the scroll bar to scroll all the way to the far end of the worksheet.

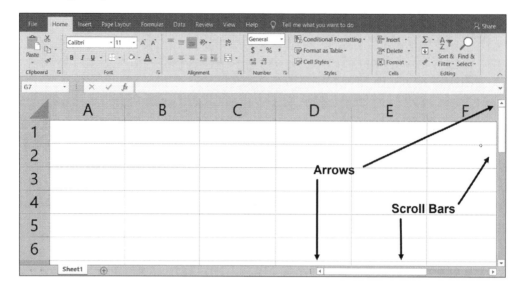

Data

I use data and information interchangeably. Whatever information you put into a worksheet is your data.

Table

I may also refer to a table of data or data table on occasion. This is just a combination of rows and columns that contain information.

This should not be confused with the Word version of a table which is a set aside combination of rows and columns. Even if you create a table in Excel with a border around the edges and nothing else in the document, you're still working in a worksheet that contains a set number of columns and rows that never changes no matter what you do.

Select

If I tell you to "select" cells, that means to highlight them. If the cells are next to each other, you can just left-click on the first one and drag the cursor (move your mouse or finger on the trackpad) until all of the cells are highlighted. When this happens, they'll all be surrounded by a dark box like below.

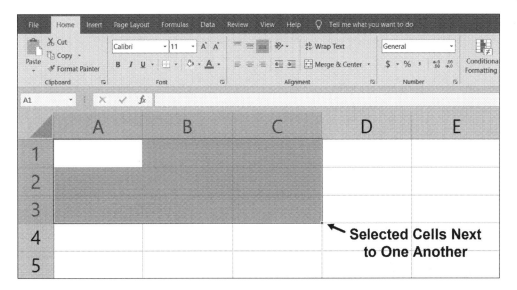

Selected Cells Next to One Another

If the cells aren't next to each other, then what you do is left-click on the first cell, hold down the Ctrl key (bottom left on my keyboard), left-click on the next cell, hold down the Ctrl key, left-click on the next cell, etc. until you've selected all the cells you want.

The cells you've already selected will be shaded in gray. The last cell you selected will be surrounded by a dark border.

In the image below cells A1, C1, A3, and C3 are selected. Cell C3 was selected last.

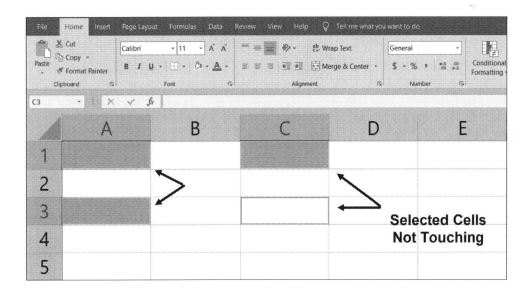

Selected Cells Not Touching

Cursor

If you didn't know this one already, it's what moves around when you move the mouse (or use the trackpad). In Excel it often looks like a three-dimensional squat cross or it will look like one of a couple of varieties of arrow. (You can open Excel and move the arrow to where the column and row labels are to see what I mean.) The different shapes the cursor takes represent different functions that are available.

Arrow

If I say that you can "arrow" to something that just means to use the arrow keys to navigate from one cell to another. For example, if you enter information in Cell A1 and hit Enter, that moves your cursor down to cell A2. If instead you wanted to move to the right to Cell B1, you could do so by using the right arrow.

Dropdown

I will occasionally refer to a dropdown or dropdown menu. This is generally a list of potential choices that you can select from. The existence of the list is indicated by an arrow next to the first available selection. You can see a number of examples in the image below.

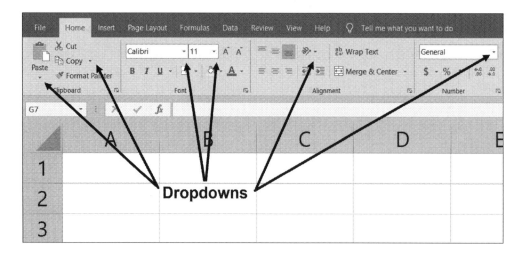

I will also sometimes refer to the list of options you see when you click on a dropdown arrow as the dropdown menu.

Dialogue Box

Dialogue boxes are pop-up boxes that contain a set of available options and appear when you need to provide additional information or make additional choices. For example, this is the Find and Replace dialogue box which appears when you select the Replace option from the Editing section of the Home tab:

Absolute Basics

It occurs to me that there are a few absolute basics to using Excel that we should cover before we get into things like formatting.

Opening an Excel File

To start a brand new Excel file, I simply click on Excel from my applications menu or the shortcut icon I have on my computer's taskbar, and it opens a new Excel file for me.

If you're opening an existing Excel file, you can either go to the folder where the file is saved and double-click on the file name, or you can (if Excel is already open) go to the File tab and choose Open from the left-hand menu.

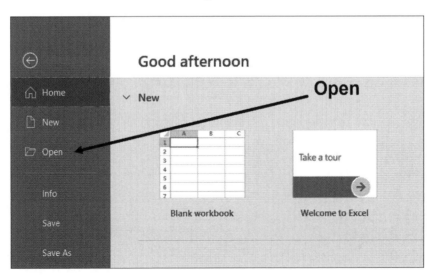

That will show you a list of Recent Workbooks. If it includes the one you're looking for, you can just click on it once and it will open.

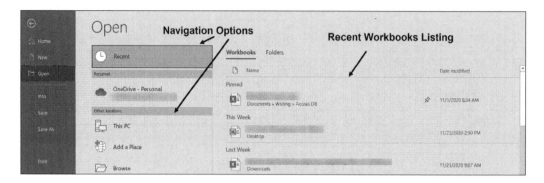

If you don't see the file you're looking for, you can click on the list of navigation options in between the left-hand menu and the list of Recent Workbooks and navigate to where the file is stored. When I click on This PC it gives me a list of recently used folders. If the document I want isn't in one of those folders, I can use the Browse option instead. If you use the cloud, OneDrive is also an option.

Excel may show an error message when you open some files in Excel. The one I usually see is about Excel opening a file in Protected View because it's a file I didn't create.

Don't panic, it's fine. You can see the contents without doing anything or if you need to edit just click on Enable Editing as long as you trust the source of the file.

Saving an Excel File

Excel has two options for saving a file, Save and Save As. If you have an existing file that's already been saved before and no changes to make to its name, location, or type, you can use Ctrl + S or click on the small computer disc image in the top left corner to save the file once more. Simply closing the file will also prompt Excel to ask if you'd like to save your changes to the document.

If the file you are saving is an .xlsx file type, you should really see nothing else at that point. The file is saved when you use Ctrl + S or the disc image or click on Save when you close the file..

If the file you're trying to save is an .xls file type (so an older file type) or another type of file like a .csv file or a .txt file, you may see an additional message when you try to Save about compatibility. The dialogue box that appears will tell you the issue that saving the file as-is will create and you need to decide whether that's okay or whether to go back into the file and fix the issue before saving.

(Usually I can just say continue when this happens because it opened from the old format and is saving to the old format so isn't going to be a huge concern as long as I didn't do some new fancy analysis in the meantime.)

All of the above options will also work for a brand new file, but they will bring up a dialogue box asking what you want to name the file and where you want to save it.

Clicking on More Options from that dialogue box will take you to the Save As screen that can also be reached by clicking on Save As on the left-hand side after clicking on the File tab.

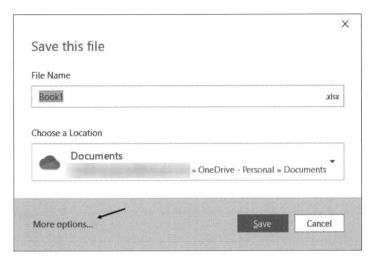

With the Save As option available under the File tab, Excel will ask you to choose which folder to save the file into. You can either choose from the list of recent folders on the right-hand side, or navigate to the folder you want using the locations listing on the left-hand side (OneDrive, This PC, and Browse).

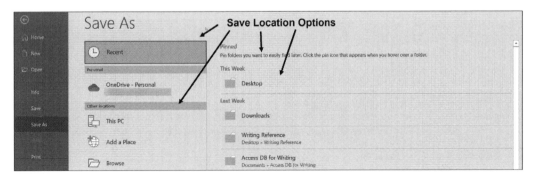

Once you choose Browse or select a folder, a dialogue box will appear where you can name the file and choose its format.

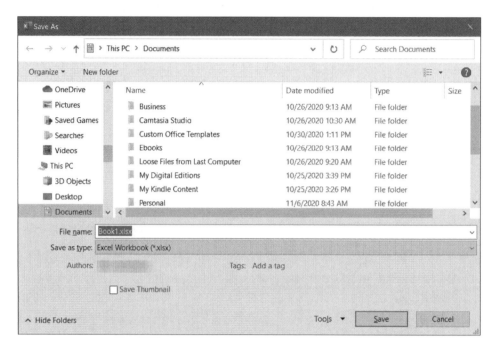

You can also navigate to a different file location at this point if you're more comfortable working in the Save As dialogue box.

To change the file type, click on the dropdown arrow for the option next to Save As Type under the File Name.

The default in Excel 2019 is to save to an .xlsx file type. Know that this file type is not compatible with versions of Excel prior to Excel 2007. At this point you're probably safe working with the default .xlsx file type, but this can be an issue with older versions of the program.

If you routinely work with someone who has an older version of Excel I would highly recommend saving your files as Excel 97-2003 Workbook .xls files instead so that you don't create a file that won't work for them. It's much easier to initially save down to an older version than try to do it after the fact.

As mentioned above, if functionality or content will be lost by saving to the format you chose, Excel will generate a warning message about compatibility when you save the file.

If you have an existing file that you want to rename, save to a new location, or save as a new file type, use the Save As option by going to the File tab and choosing Save As from there.

Deleting an Excel File

You can't delete an Excel file from within Excel. You'll need to navigate to the folder where the file is stored and delete the file there without opening it.

To do this, first, click on the file name. (Only enough to select it. Make sure you haven't double-clicked and highlighted the name which will then try to rename the file.) Then choose Delete from the menu at the top of the screen, or right-click and choose Delete from the dropdown menu.

Renaming an Excel File

You might want to rename an Excel file at some point. You can Save As and choose a new name for the file, but that will mean you now have two versions of the file, one with the old name and one with the new name.

A better option is to navigate to the folder where you have the file saved, click on it once to highlight the file, click on it a second time to highlight the name, and then type in the new name you want to use. If you do it that way, there will only be one version of the file, the one with the name you wanted.

However, if you do rename a file by changing the name in the source folder, know that you can't then access it from the Recent Workbooks listing under Open file. Even though it might be listed there, Excel won't be able to find it because it no longer has that name. (Same thing happens if you move a file from the location it was in when you were last working on it. I often run into this by moving a file into a new subfolder when I suddenly get inspired to organize my records.)

Closing an Excel File

When you're done with Excel you're going to want to close your file. The easiest way to do so is to click on the X in the top right corner of the screen. Or you can use Alt +F4. (If you use Alt+F4 this will only work if the F functions are set up to be the default keys on your keyboard.)

To just close a worksheet but keep Excel open you can use Ctrl + W.

Navigating Excel

The next thing we're going to discuss is basic navigation within Excel. These are all things you can do that don't involve inputting, formatting, or manipulating your data.

Basic Navigation Within A Worksheet

Excel will automatically open into cell A1 of Sheet1 for a new Excel file. For an existing file it will open in the cell and worksheet where you were when you last saved the file. (This means it can also open with a set of cells already highlighted if that's what you were doing when you last saved the file.)

Within a worksheet, it's pretty basic to navigate.

You can click into any cell you can see in the worksheet using your mouse or trackpad. Just place your cursor over the cell and left-click.

From the cell where you currently are (which will be outlined with a dark border), you can use the up, down, left, and right arrow keys to move one cell at a time in any of those directions.

You can also use the tab key to move one cell at a time to the right and the shift and tab keys combined (shift + tab) to move one cell at a time to the left.

To see other cells in the worksheet that aren't currently visible, you can use the scroll bars on the right-hand side or the bottom of the worksheet. The right-hand scroll bar will let you move up and down. The bottom scroll bar will let you move right or left. Just remember that the bars themselves will only let you move as far as you've entered data or the default workspace. You need to use the arrows at the ends of the scroll bars to move farther than that.

For worksheets with lots of data in them, click on the scroll bar and drag it to move quickly to the beginning or end of the data. To move one view's worth at a time, click in the blank gray space around the actual scroll bar.

If you're using the scroll bars to navigate a large amount of data or records, know that until you click into a new cell with your mouse or trackpad you will still be in the last cell where you had clicked or made an edit. So be sure to click into one of the cells you see rather than try to immediately type or to use the tab or arrow keys to navigate. (I run into this frequently when I have Freeze Panes on and then try to use an arrow key to move from the first row of column labels into my data, forgetting that the data I'm actually seeing is hundreds of rows away from that top row. Don't worry, we'll discuss Freeze Panes later.)

F2

If you click in a cell and hit the F2 key, this will take you to the end of the contents of the cell. This can be very useful when you need to edit the contents of a cell or to work with a formula in that cell. I use it often enough that every time I get a new computer I make sure that the F keys are the default rather than the volume controls, etc.

Adding a New Worksheet

When you open a new Excel file in Excel 2019, you'll have one worksheet you can use named Sheet1.

If you need another worksheet, simply click on the + symbol in a circle next to that Sheet1 tab.

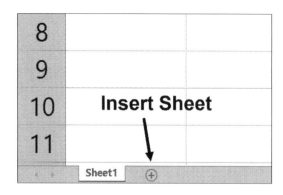

If you already have multiple worksheets in your workbook, the + sign will be located to the right of the last worksheet.

You can also go to the Home tab under the Cells section and left-click the arrow under Insert and then select Insert Sheet from the dropdown menu there.

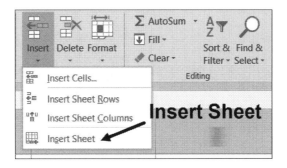

Deleting a Worksheet

Sometimes you'll add a worksheet and then realize you don't want it anymore. It's easy enough to delete. Just right-click on the name of the worksheet you want to delete and choose the Delete option from the dropdown menu (which will actually drop upward.)

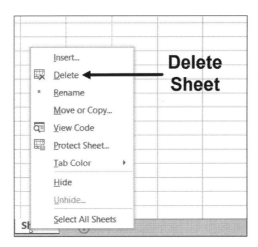

If there was any data in the worksheet you're trying to delete, Excel will give you a warning message to that effect in a dialogue box.

If you don't care, click Delete. If you do care and want to cancel the deletion, click Cancel.

Another way to delete a worksheet is to go to the Cells section in the Home tab, left-click on the arrow next to Delete, and choose Delete Sheet from the dropdown menu there.

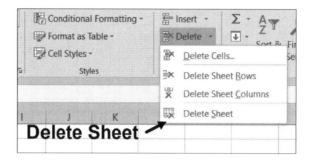

Be sure you want to delete any worksheet you choose to delete, because you can't get it back later. This is one place where undo (which we'll discuss later) will not work.

Basic Navigation Between Worksheets

Once you have multiple worksheets in your workbook, you can navigate between them by either clicking on the name of the worksheet you want at the bottom of the screen or by using Ctrl + Page Up to move one worksheet to the left or Ctrl + Page Dn to move one worksheet to the right.

The Ctrl shortcuts do not loop around, so if you're at the first worksheet and want to reach the last one you need to use Ctrl + Page Dn to move through all of the other worksheets to get there.

Or you could just click onto the last one like I do and skip the ctrl shortcut.

If you have too many worksheets to see their names on one screen, use the arrows at the left-hand side of the worksheet names or the … at the ends (when visible) to see the rest. The … will take you all the way to the beginning or the end.

Insert a Cell in a Worksheet

Sometimes you will just want to insert one cell or a small handful of cells into your worksheet. This will happen when you already have data entered into the worksheet and realize that you need to put additional data in the midst of what you already have entered.

(Because, remember, Excel worksheets have a fixed unchanging number of cells based upon the numbers of rows and columns they contain. So inserting a cell isn't really inserting a cell so much as telling Excel to move all of your information from that point over or down to make room for the new cell or cells.)

To insert a cell or cells, select the cell or cell range where you want to insert your new blank cells, right-click, and choose Insert from the dropdown menu.

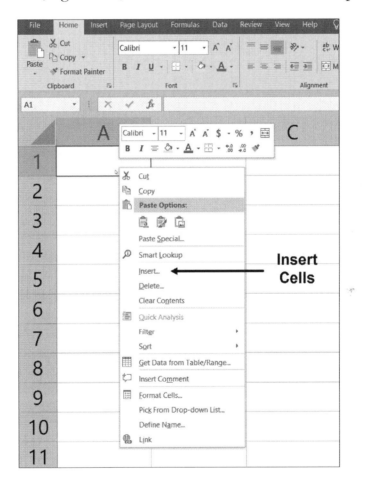

You'll be given four choices, Shift Cells Right, Shift Cells Down, Entire Row, and Entire Column. (See dialogue box screenshot on next page.)

Shift Cells Right will insert your cell or range of cells by moving every other cell in that row or rows to the right to make room for the new cell or cells.

Shift Cells Down will insert your cell or range of cells by moving every other cell in that column or columns down to make room.

Entire row will insert an entire new row at that point.

Entire column will insert an entire new column at that point.

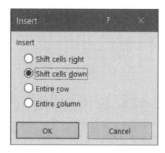

If you have a range of cells selected when you choose entire row or entire column then that number of rows or columns will be inserted. So, select three rows and choose entire row and three new rows will be inserted. Select three columns and choose entire column and three new columns will be inserted.

(Be sure that the cells you select and the option you choose make sense given the other data you've already entered in the worksheet. Sometimes I find that I need to actually highlight a larger range of cells and insert cells for all of them in order to keep the rest of my data aligned.)

You can also highlight the cell or cells where you want to insert and then go to the Cells section of the Home tab where it says Insert and choose Insert Cells from the dropdown to bring up the Insert dialogue box. Just clicking on Insert instead of using the dropdown menu will automatically insert a cell or cells by moving everything down.

There is also a control shortcut for this one (Ctrl+Shift+=) but I never use it.

Insert a Column or Row

From the above discussion you can see that it's also possible to insert an entire row or column into your existing data.

The easiest way to do so is to select the row or column where you want your new row or column to go, right-click, and choose Insert from the dropdown menu.

(To select a row or column you just click on either the letter of the column or the number of the row. You'll know it worked if all cells in that row or column are then shaded gray showing that they've been selected.)

For columns, when a new column is inserted all of your data will shift to the right one column. For rows all of your data will shift down one row. So data in Column C will move to Column D and data in Row 2 will move to Row 3.

As we saw above, you can also just right-click in a single cell, choose Insert, and then choose Entire Row or Entire Column from the Insert Dialogue Box.

Another option is to click in a cell or highlight the row or column where you want to insert and then go to the Cells section of the Home tab and use the Insert dropdown to choose Insert Sheet Rows or Insert Sheet Columns.

Delete a Cell in a Worksheet

Deleting a cell or range of cells in a worksheet is a lot like inserting one. Select the cell or cells you want to delete, right-click, and choose Delete from the dropdown menu.

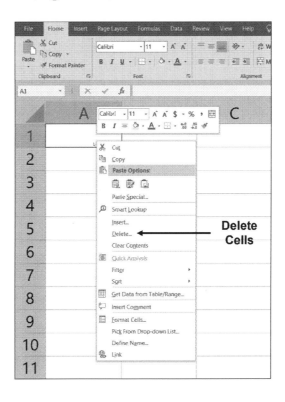

Next, choose whether to shift cells up or left, keeping in mind that when you remove a cell everything will have to move to fill in the empty space it leaves.

Double-check to make sure that deleting that cell or range of cells didn't change the layout of the rest of your data. (I sometimes find I need to delete more than one cell to keep things uniform.)

(Note that you can also delete an entire row or column this way as well just like you could with inserting.)

Another option is to highlight the cell(s) you want to delete, and then go to the Cells section of the Home tab where it says Delete and choose the delete option you want from there. Just clicking on Delete will shift the remaining data upward one row. Using the dropdown to choose Delete Cells will open the Delete dialogue box which gives you the option to shift the remaining data to the left.

Delete a Column or Row

Same as with inserting a column or row. The easiest option is to highlight the entire row or column you want to delete, right-click, and select Delete.

You can also highlight the row or column and then go to the Cells section of the Home tab where it says Delete and choose the delete option you want from the dropdown there. Or you can click into one cell, right-click, select Delete, and then choose Entire Row or Entire Column from the dialogue box.

Renaming A Worksheet

The default name for worksheets in Excel are Sheet1, Sheet2, Sheet3, etc. They're not useful for much of anything, and if you have information in more than one worksheet, you're going to want to rename them to something that lets you identify which worksheet is which.

If you double left-click on a worksheet name (on the tab at the bottom) it will highlight in gray and you can then delete the existing name and replace it with whatever you want by simply typing in the new worksheet name.

You can also right-click on the tab name and choose Rename from the dropdown menu and it will highlight the tab name in gray and let you type in your new name that way as well.

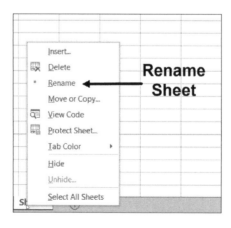

A worksheet name cannot be more than 31 characters long, be blank, contain the forward slash, the back slash, a question mark, a star, a colon, or brackets (/ \ ? * : [ ]), begin or end with an apostrophe, or be named History.

Don't worry about memorizing that. In Excel 2019 it won't let you type the prohibited characters or let you type more characters than the limit allows.

Moving or Copying Worksheet

There may be times that you want to move a worksheet around, so change the order of the worksheets in a workbook or even move that particular worksheet into a new Excel workbook. I've also on more than one occasion wanted to take a copy of a worksheet in one workbook and put that copy into a different workbook.

To move a worksheet within an Excel workbook, click on the name of the worksheet you want to move, hold down that click, and drag the worksheet to the new position you want for it. While you're dragging you should see what looks like a little piece of paper under your cursor arrow. This shows you where you're dragging the worksheet to. Once it's where you want it, just release the click and it should drop into the new position.

To move a worksheet to a new workbook or to copy one to a new workbook is basically the same. Right-click on the worksheet name and choose Move or Copy from the dropdown menu.

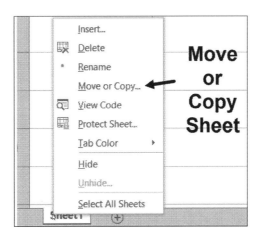

This will open the Move or Copy dialogue box. There are three options available in the dialogue box. The first is "To Book" which is where you select the file you'd like to move your worksheet to. If you're just copying the worksheet and keeping that copy within the current workbook, then leave this option alone. If you want to move or copy the worksheet to a new workbook, then use the dropdown menu to select that new workbook. Your options will consist of all of the workbooks you have open at the time as well as an option to create a new workbook.

The second choice you have is where to place the copied or moved worksheet. This is in a box labeled Before Sheet and it will list all of the current worksheets in the selected workbook. Choose the (move to end) option to place the worksheet at the end.

If you are copying the worksheet and not just moving it, so you want the original version to stay where it is but to use a copy in either that workbook or another, be sure to check the Create a Copy checkbox at the bottom.

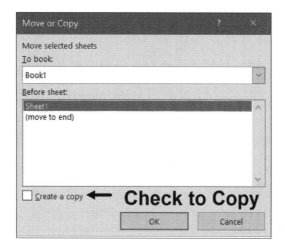

Click OK when you're done and the worksheet will be moved or copied.

Inputting Your Data

At its most basic, inputting your data is very simple. Click in the cell where you want to input information and type. But there are some tricks to it that you'll want to keep in mind.

First, let's take a step back and talk about one of the key strengths of using Excel and that's the ability to sort or filter your data. For example, I publish books, and every month I get reports from the places where my books are published listing all of the sales of my books at those locations. But what if I only care about the sales of book A? How can I see those if I have a couple hundred rows of information about various books in the report they've given me?

Well, if the site where I sold those books is nice and helpful and they understand data analysis, they've given me my sales listings in an Excel worksheet with one header row at the top and then one row for each sale or for each book. If they've done that, then I can very easily filter my data on the title column and see just the entries related to a specific title. If they haven't, then I'm stuck deleting rows of information I don't need to get to the data I want.

Which is all a roundabout way of saying that you can input your data any way you want, but if you follow some key data principles you'll have a lot more flexibility in what you can do with that data once it's entered.

Those principles are:

1. Use the first row of your worksheet to label your data.

2. List all of your data in continuous rows after that first row without including any subtotals or subheadings or anything that isn't your data.

3. To the extent possible, format your data in such a way that it can be analyzed. (So rather than put in a free-text field, try to use a standardized

list of values instead. See below. Column E, which uses a 1 to 5 point ranking scale, is better for analysis than Column D, which is a free text field where anyone can say anything.)

4. Standardize your values. Customer A should always be listed as Customer A. United States should always be United States not USA, U.S.A., or America.

5. Store your raw data in one location; analyze or correct it elsewhere.

I get into all of this much more in a book called *Data Principles for Beginners*, but that's the basic gist of how to best store data in an Excel worksheet if you're planning to do any analysis on it.

Here's an example of how it looks.

	A	B	C	D	E	F	G	H
1	Customer Name	Invoice	Date	Customer Feedback	Customer Satisfaction Score		Row 1 Identifies	
2	Customer Name A	$110	1-Jan	asbasbdasdas	1		Contents	
3	Customer Name B	$125	15-Feb	asdas	1			
4	Customer Name C	$150	7-Apr	kjjkhj	1		Other Rows	
5	Customer Name D	$225	21-Jan	adsas	4		Contain Data	
6	Customer Name E	$250	10-Sep	aiasdasd	5			

This is for data analysis, but there are many ways in which I use Excel that don't require that kind of analysis so don't follow those types of rules. My budgeting worksheet, for example, is not meant to be filtered or sorted. It's a snapshot of information that summarizes my current financial position. But my worksheet that lists all vendor payments for the year? You bet it's formatted using this approach.

So before you enter any data into your Excel file, put some time into thinking about how you want to use that data.

Is it just a visual snapshot? If so, don't worry about structuring it for sorting or filtering.

Will it be hundreds of rows of values that you want to summarize or analyze? If so, then arrange it in the way I showed above. You don't have to have Row 1 be your column headings (although it does make it easier), but wherever you do put those headings, keep everything below that point single rows of data that are all formatted and entered in the same way so that they can be compared to one another.

Okay?

Now that we've gotten that out of the way, let's discuss a few quick tricks that will make entering your data and analyzing it easier, starting with Undo and Redo.

Undo

If you enter the wrong information or perform the wrong action and want to easily undo it, hold down the Ctrl key and the Z key at the same time. (Ctrl + Z) You can do this multiple times if you want to undo multiple actions, although there are a few actions (such as deleting a worksheet) that cannot be undone.

You can also click on the left-pointing hooked arrow at the very top of the Excel workbook to undo an action. It's located in the Quick Access Toolbar right above the File and Home tabs next to where you can click on the disc image to save a file.

Clicking on the dropdown arrow next to the undo arrow will give you a list of all of the actions that you can undo at that point in time. You can then select the first action or a series of actions from there. If you want to undo something you did four actions ago, you have to undo the last three actions as well.

Undo is a life saver. If you only remember one control shortcut, make it this one. Ctrl + Z is your friend.

Redo

If you mistakenly undo something and want it back, you can hold down the Ctrl key and the Y key at the same time to redo it. (Ctrl + Y)

In the Quick Access Toolbar there is an arrow that points to the right that will be available if you just undid something which you can click on as well instead of using the control shortcut.

If you undo multiple actions at once, you can redo all of them at once as well using the Quick Access Toolbar. But again, if you want to redo actions 1, 2, and 4 you will also have to redo action 3. You can't pick and choose.

Auto-Suggested Text

If you've already typed text into a cell, Excel will suggest that text to you in subsequent cells in the same column.

For example, if you are creating a list of all the books you own (something I once tried to do and gave up after about a hundred entries), and in Cell A1 you type "science fiction", when you go to Cell A2 and type an "s", Excel will automatically suggest to you "science fiction". If you don't want to use that suggestion, then keep typing. If you do, then hit enter.

This is very convenient because instead of typing fifteen characters you only have to type one, but it only works when you have unique values for Excel to identify. If you have science fiction/fantasy and science fiction as entries in your list then it's not going to work because Excel waits until it can suggest one single option. So you'd have to type "science fiction/" before it made any suggestions in that scenario

Also, if there are empty cells between the entries you already completed and the one you're now completing and you have no other columns with completed data in them to bridge that gap and let Excel know the cells are related, Excel won't make a suggestion.

(Which means if you're going to use Auto-Suggested text it helps to have a column next to where you're inputting your data that is a numbered entries column that will let auto-complete work even if you're not entering your data row by row but are instead jumping around a bit.)

Another time this doesn't work is if you have a very long list that you've completed and the matching entry is hundreds of rows away from the one you're now completing.

Excel also doesn't make suggestions for numbers. If you have an entry that combines letters and numbers, it won't make a suggestion until you've typed at least one letter from the entry.

Despite all these apparent limitations, auto-suggested text can be very handy to use if you have to enter one of a limited number of choices over and over again and can't easily copy the information into your worksheet. It's also helpful to factor this in when deciding what your values will be. For example, I have a book *Excel for Beginners* and a book *Excel for Beginners Quiz Book*. Rather than list them that way in my advertising tracker where I have to make manual entries I list the quiz book as *Quiz Book: Excel for Beginners*. This lets me just type E or just type Q and have Excel complete the rest of both titles for me.

(We're not going to get into it in this book, but if you do have a limited list of values that you want available to enter and can't use auto-suggested text because maybe it's Widget1 and Widget2 so it won't help, then one alternate workaround would be to set up Data Validation with a list of values. Data Validation is covered in *Excel 2019 Intermediate*.)

Alright. Next.

Copying the Contents and Formatting of One Cell To Another

Copying the contents and formatting of a cell to another is something you will probably need to do often. And it is very easy to do.

First, highlight the information you want to copy, next, hold down the Ctrl and C keys at the same time (Ctrl + C), and then go to the cell where you want to put the information you copied and hit Enter.

If you want to copy the information to more than one location, instead of hitting Enter at the new cell, hold down the Ctrl and V keys at the same time (Ctrl + V) to paste.

If you use Ctrl + V, you'll see that the original cell you copied from is still surrounded by a dotted line which indicates that the information you copied is still available to be pasted into another cell. You can see this by clicking into another cell and using Ctrl + V again. It will paste the information you copied a second time.

Another way to copy is to select your information and then right-click and choose Copy from the dropdown menu. You can then use Enter, Ctrl + V, or right-click and choose Paste from the dropdown menu to paste the information.

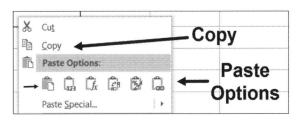

For a basic copy of the information choose the first option under Paste Options which is a clipboard with a blank piece of paper. Hold your cursor over it and you should see it described as Paste (P).

Once you're done pasting the values into new cells and want to do something else, just hit the Esc key. This will remove the dotted line from around the cell you were copying and ensure you don't accidentally paste it somewhere else. Typing text into a new cell also works to turn off the copy/paste that you've initiated.

(When in doubt in Excel using Esc is very helpful. It's kind of like an Undo function when you haven't yet done anything but have started something you don't want to finish.)

In the Clipboard section of the Home tab you can also find another set of Copy and Paste options (as well as Cut which we're about to discuss), but I almost never use them because these are tasks where learning your control shortcuts will save you a lot of time.

So, Ctrl + C to Copy, Ctrl + V to Paste, and, as we're about to learn, Ctrl + X to Cut. Memorize those and learn to use them. Trust me.

Moving the Contents of a Cell

To move selected information rather than just copy it, select the information, type Ctrl and X at the same time (Ctrl + X), click on the new location, and hit Enter or type Ctrl + V.

Unlike with copying, you can only move the contents of a cell to one new location. Once you hit Enter or use Ctrl + V that information will have moved and you cannot paste it anywhere else without first copying it from the new location.

Another option for moving your information is to highlight the information you want to move, right-click, and choose Cut from the dropdown menu and then paste your cell contents in the new location.

Copying the contents of a cell (Ctrl + C) is different from cutting and moving the contents of a cell (Ctrl + X), because when you copy the contents of a cell, (Ctrl + C), they remain in their original location. When you move the contents of a cell, (Ctrl + X), you are removing them from their original location to place them in their new location.

Note that I've been talking about Copying or Cutting information rather than cells, because you can actually click into a specific cell, highlight just a portion of the content of that cell and Copy or Cut that portion only. You do this by clicking into the cell and then going to the Formula Bar to highlight the text you want, or by clicking on a cell and then using F2 to access the contents of that cell and then the arrow keys and the Shift key to highlight the text you want.

Copying Versus Moving When It Comes to Formulas

If you're dealing with text, copying (Ctrl + C) or cutting the text (Ctrl + X) doesn't really change anything. What ends up in that new cell will be the same regardless of the method you use.

But with formulas, that's not what happens.

With formulas, moving the contents of a cell (Ctrl + X) will keep the formula the exact same as it was. So if your formula was =A2+B2 it will still be =A2+B2 in the new cell.

Copying the contents of a cell (Ctrl + C) will change the formula based upon the number of rows and columns you moved. The formula is copied relative to where it originated. If your original formula in Cell A3 is =A2+B2 and you copy it to Cell A4 (so move it one cell downward) the formula in Cell A4 will be =A3+B3. All cell references in the formula adjust one cell downward.

If you copy that same formula to Cell B3 (so one cell to the right) the formula in B3 will be =B2+C2. All cell references in the formula adjust one cell to the right.

If this doesn't make sense to you, just try it. Put some sample values in cells A2 and B2 and then experiment with Ctrl + C versus Ctrl + X.

Also, there is a way to prevent a formula from changing when you copy it using the $ sign to keep the cell references fixed. We'll talk about that next.

Copying Formulas To Other Cells While Keeping One Value Fixed

If you want to copy a formula while keeping the value of one or more of the cells fixed, you need to use the $ sign.

A $ sign in front of the letter portion of a cell location will keep the column the same but allow the row number to change. ($A1)

A $ sign in front of the number portion of a cell location will keep the row the same but allow the column to change. (A$1)

A $ sign in front of both the column and row portion will keep the referenced cell exactly the same. (A1)

This will be discussed in more detail in the manipulating data section because where it really comes up is in mathematical calculations and functions.

Paste Special

I often want to take values I've calculated in Excel and just keep the end result without keeping the formula. For example, with my advertising in the UK the values are reported to me in that currency (GBP) but I want to convert them to my currency (USD). Once I've done that, I don't need to keep the calculation because the only thing that matters for my purposes is the end value in my currency.

Other reasons to use Paste Special include wanting to copy the contents of a cell but not keep the formatting from that cell. Also, I use it to turn a series of values that are displayed across columns into a series of values that are displayed across rows, or vice versa.

The first thing to know about Paste Special is that you can only use it if you've copied (Ctrl + C) the contents of a cell or cells. It doesn't work with Cutting (Ctrl + X).

To Paste Special use the dropdown option for pasting or the dropdown option in the Clipboard section of the Home tab. You cannot use the Ctrl shortcut to paste.

So, right-click where you want to Paste and go to Paste Options or click on the dropdown arrow under Paste in the Clipboard section of the Home tab. You should see options that look like this:

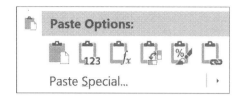

In my opinion, not all of these choices are useful. So I'm just going to highlight two of them for you.

Paste Values, the second option above which has the 123 on its clipboard, is useful for when you want the results of a formula, but don't want the formula anymore. I use this often.

It's also useful when you want the contents of a cell, but would prefer to use the formatting from the destination cell(s). For example, if you're copying from one Excel file to another.

Another way I use it is when I've run a set of calculations on my data, found my values, and now want to sort or do something else with my data and don't want to risk having the values change on me. I highlight the entire data set, copy, and then paste special-values right over the top of my existing data. (Just be sure to type Esc after you do this so that the change is fixed in place.)

Paste Transpose, the fourth option with the little arrow arcing between two pairs of cells, is very useful if you have a row of data that you want to turn into columns of data or vice versa. Just highlight the data, copy, paste-transpose, and it will automatically paste a column of data as a row or a row of data as a column.

Just be sure before you paste that there isn't any data already there that will be overwritten, because Excel won't warn you before it overwrites it.

There are more paste options available than just the six you can see above. If you click on where it says Paste Special you'll see another dropdown menu to the side with eight more options, and if you go to the bottom of that breakout menu and click on Paste Special again, it will bring up the Paste Special dialogue box which allows you to pick and choose from the various paste options. The dropdown available from the Clipboard section of the Home tab is the same as the Paste Special dropdown list of options and you can also bring up the dialogue box from there by choosing Paste Special at the bottom.

Displaying The Contents Of A Cell As Text

Excel likes to change certain values to what it thinks you meant. So if you enter June 2015 into a cell, it will convert that entry to a date even if you intended it to be text. To see this, type June 2015 in a cell, hit enter, click back into the cell, and you'll see in the formula bar that it says 6/1/2015 and it displays as Jun-15 in the cell.

Excel also assumes that any entry that starts with a minus sign (-), an equals sign (=), or a plus sign (+) is a formula.

To keep Excel from messing with your entries, you can type a single quote mark (') before the contents of the cell. If you do that, Excel will treat whatever you enter after that as text and will keep the formatting type as General.

So if you want to have June 2015 display in a cell in your worksheet, you need to type 'June 2015.

If you want to have

- Item A

display in a cell, you need to type it as:

'- Item A

The single quote mark is not visible when you look at or print your worksheet. It is only visible in the formula bar when you've selected the impacted cell.

Entering a Formula Into a Cell

The discussion just above about displaying the contents of a cell as text brings up another good point. If you want Excel to treat an entry as a formula, then you need to enter the equals (=), plus (+), or negative sign (-) as your first character in the cell. So, if you type

1+1

in a cell, that will just display as text in the cell. You'll see

1+1

But if you type

+1+1

in a cell, Excel will treat that as a formula and calculate it. You'll see 2 in the cell and

=1+1

in the formula bar.

Same with if you type

$$=1+1$$

It will calculate that as a formula, display 2 in the cell, and show

$$=1+1$$

in the formula bar.
If you type

$$-1+1$$

in a cell it will treat that as a formula adding negative 1 to 1 and will show that as 0 in the cell and display

$$=-1+1$$

in the formula bar.
Best practice is to use the equals sign to start every formula since Excel converts it to using the equals sign anyway.

Including Line Breaks Within a Cell

I sometimes need to have multiple lines of text or numbers within a cell. So instead of a, b, c, I need

a
b
c

You can't just hit Enter, because if you do it'll take you to the next cell. Instead, hold down the Alt key at the same time you hit Enter. This will create a line break within the cell.

Deleting Data

If you enter information into a cell and later decide you want to delete it, you can click on that cell(s) and use the delete button on your computer's keyboard. This will remove whatever you entered in the cell without deleting the cell as well.

You can also double-click into the cell or use F2 to get to the end of the contents in the cell and then use your computer's backspace key to delete out the contents of the cell from the end. If you double-click and end up somewhere in the middle of the cell you can use the delete key to delete text to the right of your cursor.

Deleting the contents of a cell does not remove its formatting. To delete the contents of a cell as well as its formatting, go to the Editing section of the Home tab, click on the dropdown next to the Clear option, and choose Clear All.

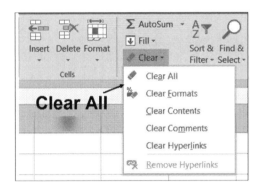

Find and Replace

Sometimes you have a big worksheet and you need to find a specific entry. An easy way to do this is to use the Find option. The easiest way to access it is to type Ctrl and F at the same time (Ctrl + F). This opens the Find dialogue box. Type what you're looking for into the "Find what" field and hit enter.

The other way to access Find is through the Editing section of the Home tab. The Find & Select option has a dropdown menu that includes Find.

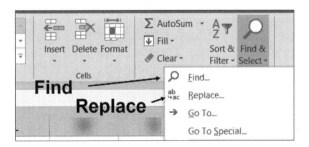

The default is for find to look in formulas as well, so if you search for "f" and have a formula that references cell F11, it will hit on that as much as it will hit on the cell that actually contains the letter f in a word.

You can change this setting under Options where it says Look In at the bottom left. Change the dropdown from Formulas to Values.

If you're looking for something in order to change it, you can use Replace instead. Type Ctrl and H (Ctrl + H) at the same time (or just Ctrl + F and then click over to the Replace tab), or you can access it through the Editing section of the Home tab.

When the Replace dialogue box opens, you'll see two lines, "Find what" and "Replace with." In the "Find what" line, type what you're looking for. In the "Replace with" line, type what to replace it with.

Be VERY careful using Replace.

Say you want to replace "hat" with "chapeau" because you've suddenly become pretentious. If you don't think this through, you will end up replacing every usage of hat, even when it's in words like "that" or "chat". So you'll end up with "tchapeau" in the middle of a sentence instead of "that" because the hat portion of "that" was replaced with "chapeau". (This probably happens in Word more than in Excel, but it's still something to be aware of.)

Replace is good for removing something like double spaces or converting formatting of a particular value, but otherwise you might want to use find and then manually correct each entry to avoid inadvertent errors.

You can get around some of these issues by clicking on Options and then using the checkboxes that let you Match Case or Match Entire Cell Contents Also, that brings up a Format dropdown that lets you search by pretty much any formatting you want such as italics, bold, underline, cell color, border, font, alignment, etc.

Searching by format can come in really handy when you need to, for example, replace italics with bold or change out a font that you used. But again, Find and Replace is used more with Microsoft Word than with Microsoft Excel in my experience.

Copying Patterns of Data

Sometimes you'll want to input data that repeats itself. Like, for example, the days of the week. Say you're putting together a worksheet that lists the date and what day of the week it is for an entire year. You could type out Monday, Tuesday, Wednesday, Thursday, Friday, Saturday, Sunday, and then copy and paste that 52 times. Or…

You could take advantage of the fact that Excel can recognize patterns. With this particular example, it looks like all it takes is typing in Monday. Do that and then go to the bottom right corner of the cell with Monday in it and position your cursor so that it looks like a small black cross. Left-click, hold that left-click down, and start to drag your cursor away from the cell. Excel should auto-complete the cells below or to the right of the Monday cell, depending on the direction you move, with the days of the week in order and repeating themselves in order for as long as you need it to.

If you're dealing with a pattern that isn't as standard as days of the week sometimes it takes a few entries before Excel can identify the pattern.

For example, if I type 1 into a cell and try to drag it, Excel just repeats the 1 over and over again. If I do 1 and then 2 and highlight both cells and start to drag from the bottom of the cell with the 2 in it, then it starts to number the next cells 3, 4, 5 etc.

You'll see the values Excel suggests for each cell as you drag the cursor through that cell, but those values won't actually appear in those cells until you're done highlighting all the cells you want to copy the pattern to and you let up on the left-click. (If that doesn't make sense, just try it a few times and you'll see what I mean.)

	E	F	G	H
1	Customer Satisfaction Score			**Excel**
2		1	1	**Copying**
3		1	2	**a Pattern**
4		1		**Into**
5		4		**Three**
6		5	5	**Cells**
7		3		

(You can combine Excel's ability to copy patterns with the AutoFill option by double-clicking in the bottom right-hand corner instead. This only works for columns and when your current column is next to a column that already has values in it for all the rows where you want to copy your pattern. (See the Manipulating Your Data section for more detail on AutoFill.)

Freeze Panes

If you have enough information in a worksheet for it to not be visible in one page, there's a chance you'll want to use freeze panes. What it does is freezes a row or rows and/or a column or columns at the top and side of your page so that even when you scroll down or to the right those rows or columns stay visible. So if you have 100 rows of information but always want to be able to see your header row, freeze panes will let you do that.

To freeze panes, go to the Window section of the View tab and click on the arrow under Freeze Panes.

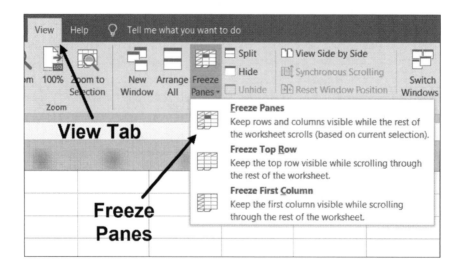

It gives you three options: Freeze Panes, Freeze Top Row, and Freeze First Column.

Those second two are pretty obvious. Choose "Freeze Top Row" and you'll always see Row 1 of your worksheet no matter how far down you scroll. Choose "Freeze First Column" and you'll always see Column A of your worksheet no matter how far to the right you scroll. When you use either of those options you are limited to just that one option, top row or first column.

However, the first option, Freeze Panes gives you the ability to freeze any number of rows AND columns at the same time. You just have to choose your cell first before choosing your freeze panes option.

So if I click on cell C4, which has three rows above it and two to the left, and then choose Freeze Panes, Excel will keep the top three rows AND the left two columns of my worksheet visible no matter where I scroll in the document.

For example, if you had customer name, city, and state in your first three columns and wanted to be able to see that information as you scrolled over to see other customer data, you could.

Or say your worksheet has a couple of rows of descriptive text and then the real row labels begin in row 5, you can click in Cell A6, choose to freeze panes, and those top five rows will always stay visible.

Freeze panes is very handy when dealing with large amounts of data. Just be careful that you don't accidentally lose where you are. If you click into a frozen row or column and then arrow down or over from there, it will take you to the next row, not the data you're seeing on the screen. So if you were looking at row 10,522 and you had the top row frozen and clicked into Row 1 for some reason and then arrowed down from there it would take you to Row 2 not Row 10,522 which is what you see on the screen. (It happens to be something I do often, so figured it was worth mentioning.)

Another thing to be cautious about with freeze panes is that you don't freeze so many rows and columns that you can't see any new data. But that would probably take quite a lot to make happen. But if you are arrowing down or to the right and can't see any new data, you just keep seeing what's already on the screen, that could be the cause.

To remove freeze panes, you can go back to the View tab and the Freeze Panes dropdown and you'll now see that that first option has become Unfreeze Panes. Just click on it and your document will go back to normal. Use that option regardless of whether you initially choose freeze panes, freeze top row, or freeze first column.

Formatting

If you're going to spend any amount of time working in Excel then you need to learn how to format cells, because inevitably your column won't be as wide as you want it to be or you'll want to have a cell with red-colored text or to use bolding or italics or something that isn't Excel's default.

That's what this section is for. It's an alphabetical listing of different things you might want to do. You can either format one cell at a time by highlighting that specific cell, format multiple cells at once by highlighting all of them and then choosing your formatting option, or format just a portion of the contents of a cell by selecting the specific text you want to format and then choosing your formatting option.

There are four main ways to format cells in Excel 2019.

The first is to use the Home tab and click the option you want from there.

The second is to right-click and select the Format Cells option from the dropdown menu which will bring up the Format Cells dialogue box.

The third is to right-click and select an option from what I refer to as the mini formatting menu (pictured below) which is located either just above or just below the dropdown menu and looks like a condensed version of the Home tab options.

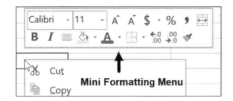

The fourth option is to use control shortcuts. These are available for some of the key formatting options such as bolding (Ctrl + B), italicizing (Ctrl + I), and underlining (Ctrl + U).

For basic formatting, I use the control shortcuts or the Home tab. If you're new to Excel you may want to use the mini formatting menu instead of the Home tab. (I don't use it because it didn't exist when I was learning Excel and it doesn't save so much time that I found it worth learning.)

For less common formatting choices, you will likely need to use the Format Cells dialogue box instead.

Aligning Your Text Within a Cell

By default, text within a cell is left-aligned and bottom-aligned. But at times you may want to adjust this. I often will center text or prefer for it to be top-aligned because it looks better to me that way when I have some column headers that are one line and others that are multiple lines.

To change the alignment in a cell or range of cells, highlight the cell(s) you want to change, and go to the Alignment section on the Home tab. There are a total of six choices which make nine possible combinations as shown below.

The six choices are on the left-hand side of the Alignment section and represented visually.

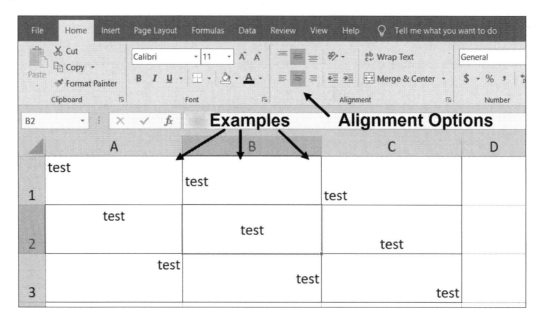

The first row has the top aligned, middle aligned, and bottom aligned options. You can choose one of these three options for your cell.

The second row has the left-aligned, centered, and right-aligned options. You can also choose one of these three options for your cell.

So you can have a cell with top-aligned and centered text or top-aligned and right-aligned text or bottom-aligned and centered text, etc. The image on the opposite page includes an example of the nine possible combinations.

You can also change the direction of your text so that it's angled or vertical.

To do so from the Home tab, click on the arrow next to the angled "ab" in the top row of the Alignment section and select one of the pre-defined options listed there.

You can choose Angle Counterclockwise, Angle Clockwise, Vertical Text, Rotate Text Up, and Rotate Text Down. (The last option, Format Cell Alignment, will bring up the Format Cells dialogue box.)

Another way to change the text alignment within a cell(s) is to highlight your cell(s) and then right-click and choose Format Cells from the dropdown menu. This will also bring up the Format Cells dialogue box. You can then go to the Alignment tab to see your available choices.

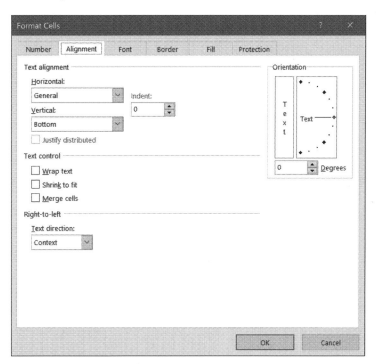

Choose from the Horizontal and Vertical dropdown menus to change the basic alignment of your text (Top, Center, Bottom, Left, Right, etc.).

The dropdown menus do have a few additional choices (like Justify and Distributed), but you generally shouldn't need them. And be wary of Fill which it seems will repeat whatever you have in that cell over and over again horizontally until it fills the cell. (Remember, if you do something you don't like, Ctrl + Z is your friend.)

On the right-hand side of the dialogue box you can also change the orientation of your text to any angle you want by entering a specified number of degrees (90 to make it vertical) or by moving the line within the Orientation box to where you want it. This is generally how I choose to angle text since I usually want an angle of about 30 degrees instead of the default choice in the Home tab which is 45 degrees.

If all you want to do is center your text, you can also use the third option in the bottom row of the mini formatting menu.

Bolding Text

You can bold text in a number of ways.

First, highlight the content you want bolded and then type Ctrl and B (Ctrl + B) at the same time. This is my preferred method.

Second, highlight your content and click on the large capital B in the Font section of the Home tab or in the bottom left row of the mini formatting menu.

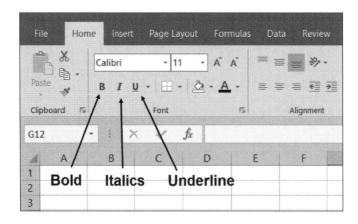

Third, you can highlight the cell(s) you want to bold and then right-click and choose Format Cells from the dropdown menu. Once you're in the Format Cells dialogue box, go to the Font tab and choose Bold from the Font Style options.

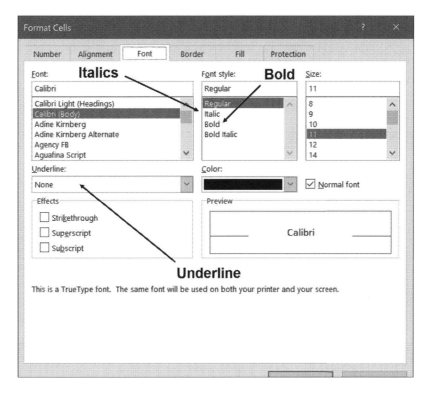

If you want text that is both bolded and italicized, choose Bold Italic.

To remove bolding from text or cells that already have it, highlight the bolded portion and then type Ctrl + B or click on the large capital B in the Font section of the Home tab or the mini formatting menu.(If you happen to highlight text that is only partially bolded you may have to do it twice to remove the bold formatting since the first time it will apply it to the rest of the text.)

Borders Around Cells

It's nice to have borders around your data to keep the information in each cell distinct, especially if you're going to print your document.

There are two main ways to add borders around a cell or set of cells. First, you can highlight the cells you want to place a border around and then go to the Font section on the Home tab and choose from the Borders dropdown option. It's a four-square grid with an arrow next to it that's located between the U used for underlining and the color bucket used for filling a cell with color.

Click on the arrow next to the grid to see your available options, and then choose the type of border you want.

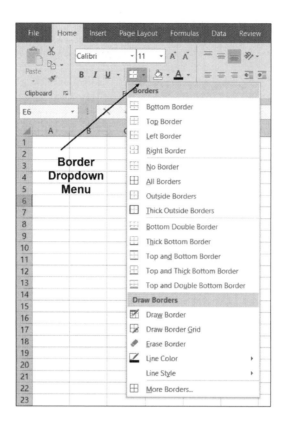

If you just want a simple border all around the cells and between multiple cells click on the All Borders option.

To adjust line thickness or line colors use the options in the Draw Borders section at the bottom, but be sure to choose your colors and line style *before* you choose your border type because the color and line type you choose will only apply to borders you draw after that.

You can also combine border types to get the appearance you want. For example, you could choose All Borders for the entire set of cells and then Thick Box Border to put a darker outline around the perimeter.

Your second choice for adding a border to your cells is to highlight the cells where you want to place a border and then right-click and select Format Cells from the dropdown menu.

When the Format Cells dialogue box appears, go to the Border tab and choose your border style, type, and color from there. (See image on next page.)

There are three Preset options at the top. If you want a basic outline or inside lines, just click on that option. To clear what you've done and start over you can select None from the Presets section.

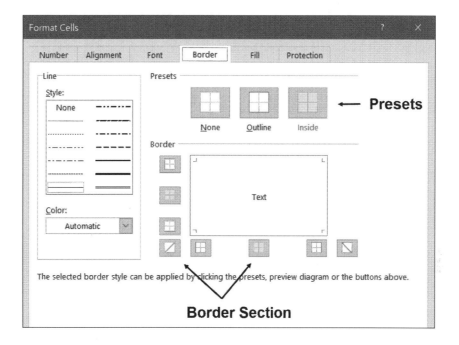

The Border section of the dialogue box allows you to pick and choose which lines you want to have in your cells, including diagonal lines. Simply click on the choice(s) you want.

You will see a preview of how it will appear in that Text box in the center section of the dialogue box.

You can click on more than one of the lines in the Border section. So you could have, for example, a top and bottom border, but nothing else.

If you want to change the style of a line or its color from the default, you can do so in the Line section on the left-hand side, but be sure to do so before you select where you want your lines to appear.

If you forget to change the style or color first, change it then just select the line placement again and it will apply the new style and/or color.

The fact that it works this way allows you to have multiple line styles or colors on a single cell which can come in handy at times.

Coloring a Cell (Fill Color)

You can color (or fill) an entire cell with almost any color you want. To do this, highlight the cell(s) you want to color, go to the Font section of the Home tab, and click on the dropdown arrow for the paint bucket that has a colored line under it. (The color will be bright yellow by default but will change as you use the tool.) You can also use the mini formatting menu where the fill color icon is the fourth in the bottom row.

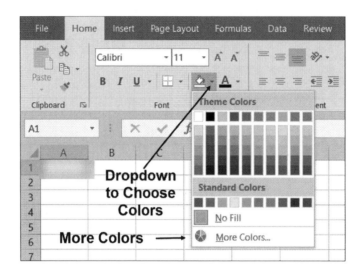

Either option will bring up a dropdown menu with 70 different colors to choose from, including the theme colors which consist of ten columns of color with six shades per color.

If you want to use any of the seventy colors you can see in the dropdown, just click on it.

If none of those colors work for you, or you need to use a specific corporate color, click on More Colors at the bottom of the dropdown menu.

This will bring up a Colors dialogue box. The first tab of that box looks like a honeycomb and has a number of colors you can choose from by clicking into the honeycomb.

The second tab is the Custom tab. It has a rainbow of colors that you can click on and also allows you to enter specific RGB or HSL values to get the exact color you need. (If you have a corporate color palette, they should give you the values for each of the corporate colors.)

On the Custom tab, you can also click and drag the arrow on the right-hand side to darken or lighten your color.

With both tabs, you can see the color you've chosen in the bottom right corner. If you like your choice, click on OK. If you don't want to add color to a cell after all, choose Cancel.

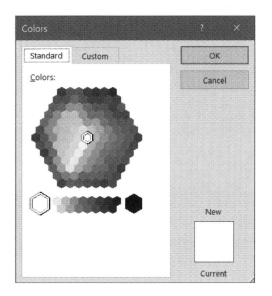 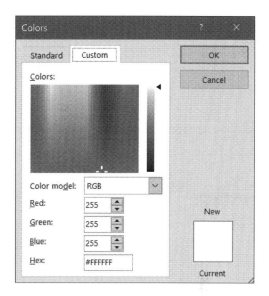

Column Width (Adjusting)

If your columns aren't the width you want, you have three options for adjusting them.

First, you can right-click on the column and choose Column Width from the dropdown menu. When the box showing you the current column width appears, enter a new column width.

Second, you can place your cursor to the right side of the column name—it should look like a line with arrows on either side—and then left-click and hold while you move the cursor to the right or the left until the column is as wide as you want it to be.

Or, third, you can place your cursor on the right side of the column name and double left-click. This will make the column as wide or as narrow as the widest text currently in that column. (Usually. Sometimes this one has a mind of its own.)

To adjust all column widths in your document at once, you can highlight the entire worksheet and then double-left click on any column border and it will adjust each column to the contents in that column. (Usually. See comment above.)

To have uniform column widths throughout your worksheet, highlight the whole worksheet, right-click on a column, choose Column Width, and set your column width. Highlighting the whole worksheet and then left-clicking and dragging one column to the desired width will also work.

(We cover it later, but to select the entire worksheet you can click in the top left corner at the intersection of the columns and rows. Or you can use Ctrl + A.)

Currency Formatting

In addition to applying basic formatting like bold, italics, and underline, Excel can also apply more complex formatting such as currency formatting or date formatting. The first of these we're going to cover is currency formatting. There are actually two default options for formatting numbers in Excel so that they look like currency notation such as $25.00. They are Accounting and Currency.

Excel defaults to the Accounting option which places the $ sign to the left-hand side of the cell even when the numbers don't fill the cell.

I tend to prefer the Currency option which keeps the $ sign with the numbers but that's because I'm usually only using this for a small range of values that are about the same size.

To apply the default Accounting format to your cells, highlight them, and then go to the Number section of the Home tab or the mini formatting menu, and click on the $ sign.

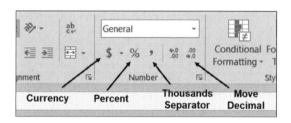

You can also use the dropdown menu in the Number section of the Home tab (which by default shows General) to choose either the Currency or Accounting format.

The final formatting option is to highlight the cell(s), right-click, choose the Format Cells option from the dropdown menu, go to the Number tab of the Format Cells dialogue box, and choose either Currency or Accounting from there.

Date Formatting

Excel can also format your entries as dates. Doing so will allow Excel to use those dates in calculations. But sometimes Excel has a mind of its own about how to format dates.

For example, if I type in 1/1 for January 1st, Excel will show it as 1-Jan and immediately turn it into a date in the current year. It may means the same thing as what I wanted, but if I'm going to display a current year date I would rather it display as 1/1/2020. That means I need to change the formatting.

One option is to click on the cell(s) with your date in it, go to the Number section on the Home tab, click on the dropdown menu, and choose either Short Date or Long Date.

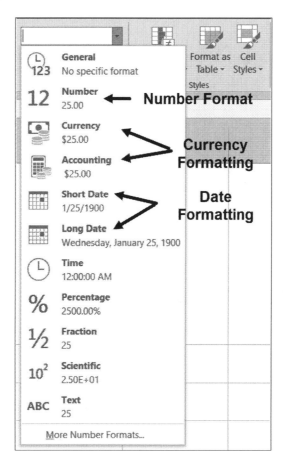

If you select a cell or range of cells where the first cell already has a number in it, you will see examples of what the format will look like when you choose it. In the example above it's showing what the number 25 will look like in each format.

I prefer Short Date because I don't really need to see the day of the week named as well, which is what Long Date does.

Another option, and the one I probably use more for this, is to highlight your cell(s), right click, choose Format Cells from the dropdown menu, go to the

Number tab of the Format Cells dialogue box, and choose your date format from there by clicking on Date and then selecting one of the numerous choices it provides.

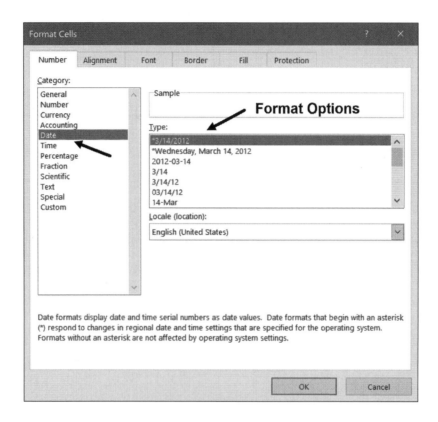

Keep in mind when selecting date formats that different countries write dates in different ways. So in the United States if I write 3/1/20 that means March 1, 2020 but in other countries that can mean January 3, 2020. You can see that the first couple of date options listed in the dialogue box will adjust for regional differences on different computers, but sometimes it's better to choose a spelled-out date to avoid any confusion.

And, just to reiterate because it's been an issue for me in the past, as mentioned above, Excel will always assign a year to a date no matter what you have it display or what information you provide. Always. So if that matters to you, be sure to control that information yourself.

Font Choice and Size

In Excel 2019 the default font choice is Calibri and the default font size is 11 point. You may have strong preferences about what font you use or work for a company that uses specific fonts for its brand or just want some variety in terms of font size or type within a specific document. In that case, you will need to change your font.

There are multiple ways to do this.

First, you can highlight your selection, go to the Font section on the Home tab, and select a different font or font size from the dropdown menus there.

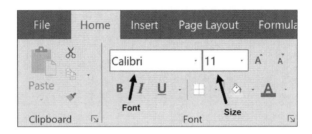

You also have the option there to increase or decrease the font one size at a time by clicking on the A's with little arrows off to the right-hand side of the dropdowns.

The same choices are also available on the left side of the first row of the mini formatting menu.

You can also highlight the cells or text you want to change, right-click, and choose Format Cells from the dropdown menu, and then go to the Font tab and choose your Font and Size from the listed values there. (I almost never find myself needing to use this option since the Home tab is so convenient.)

With any of the above options you can also choose a font size that isn't listed by clicking into the font size box and typing the value you want. So if you want a font size of 13 or 15, etc. you can just type it in.

Font Color

The default color for all text in Excel is black, but you can change that if you want or need to. (For example, if you've colored a cell with a darker color you may want to consider changing the font color to white to make the text in that cell more visible.)

You have multiple options here as well.

First, you can highlight the cells or the specific text you want to change, go to the Font section on the Home tab, and click on the arrow next to the A with a line under it. (The line is red by default but changes as you use this option.)

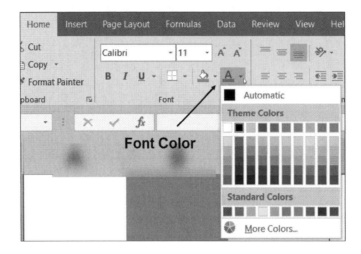

You can then choose from one of the 70 colors that are listed, and if those aren't enough of a choice you can click on More Colors and select your color from the Colors dialogue box. (See Coloring a Cell for more detail about that option.)

Second, you can use the fifth option in the bottom row of the mini formatting menu.

Third, you can highlight your selected text, right-click and choose Format Cells from the drop-down menu, go to the Font tab of the Format Cells dialogue box, and then click on the dropdown menu under Color which will bring up the same seventy color options and the ability to choose More Colors and add a custom color instead. Again, not an option I use often since the Home tab option is so convenient.

Italicizing Text

To add italics to a selection, highlight your selection and hold down the Ctrl key and the I key at the same time. (Ctrl + I)

Or you can highlight what you want italicized, and click on the slanted I in the Font section on the Home tab (see image under the Bolding description) or the bottom row of the mini formatting menu.

Another option is to highlight your selection, right-click, choose Format Cells from the dropdown menu, go to the Font tab of the Format Cells dialogue box, and choose Italic from the Font Style options.

As mentioned before, you can italicize just part of the text in a cell by only selecting that portion and then using one of the methods above.

To remove italics from text or cells that already have it, you follow the exact same steps. (Highlight your selection and then type Ctrl + I or click on the slanted I in the Font section on the Home tab or the mini formatting menu.) You may need to do it twice if your selection was not fully italicized already.

Merge & Center

Merge & Center is a specialized command that can come in handy when you're working with a table where you want a header that spans multiple columns of data.

If you're going to merge and center text, make sure that the text you want to keep is in the top-most and left-most of the cells you plan to merge and center. Data in the other cells that are being merged will be deleted. (You'll get a warning message to this effect if you have values in any of the other cells.)

You can merge cells across columns and/or down rows. So you could, for example, merge cells that span two columns and two rows into one big cell while keeping all of the other cells in those columns and rows separate.

To merge and center, highlight all of the cells you want to merge. Next, go to the Alignment section of the Home tab and choose Merge & Center. You can also find the Merge & Center option in the top right corner of the mini formatting menu.

Choosing Merge & Center will combine your selected cells into one large cell and center the contents from the topmost, left-most cell that was merged across the selection and then bottom-align the remaining text.

The Home tab also has a dropdown menu that includes additional options.

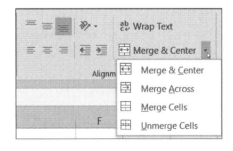

Merge Across will merge the cells across each individual row of the selected range rather than create one giant merged cell.

Merge Cells merges the cells into one cell but places the resulting text in the bottom right corner instead of the center.

Also, if you ever need to unmerge merged cells (like I do with one of my sales reports I receive) you can do so by selecting the Unmerge Cells option from the Merge & Center dropdown in the Home tab.

You can also Merge Cells by highlighting the cells, right-clicking, selecting the Format Cells option, going to the Alignment tab in the Format Cells dialogue box, and then choosing to Merge Cells from there. If you choose that option, you have to center the text separately.

A quick warning: Don't merge and center your cells if you plan to do a lot of data analysis with what you've input because it will mess with your ability to filter, sort, or use pivot tables. It's really for creating a finalized, pretty-looking report.

Number Formatting

Sometimes when you copy data into Excel it doesn't format it the way you want. For example, I have a report I receive that includes ISBN numbers which are 10- or 13- digit numbers. When I copy those into Excel, it sometimes displays them in Scientific number format ($9.78E+12$) as opposed to as a normal number.

To change the formatting of your data to a number format, you have a few options.

First, you can highlight the cell(s) and go to the Number section of the Home tab. From the drop-down menu choose Number. (Sometimes General will work as well.)

That will then convert your entries to numbers with two decimal places but no commas. So 100.00 instead of 100.

You can also click on the comma right below the dropdown to create a number with two decimal places and commas separating the thousands, hundred thousands, millions, etc.

You can then use the zeroes with arrows next to them that are located right below the drop-down box to adjust how many decimal places to display.

The one with the right-pointing arrow will reduce the number of decimal places. The one with the left-pointing arrow will increase them.

Second, the mini formatting menu has an option to format a cell as a number with commas for the thousands, hundred thousands, millions, etc. and will display with two decimal places.

To use it, select your cell(s), right-click, and from the mini formatting menu click on the comma in the top row on the right.

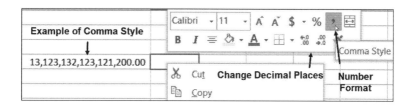

To adjust your decimal places then click on the zeroes with arrows under them in the bottom row. You can see an example of what the default looks like on the left-hand side of the image above.

Finally, you can highlight the cell(s), right-click, select Format Cells from the dropdown, go to the Number tab in the Format Cells dialogue box, choose Number on the left-hand side listing, and then in the middle choose your number of decimal places and how you want your negative numbers to display.

If I'm working with negative numbers a lot I'll use this option so that I can display my negative numbers either as red text or with ( ) around them.

You can also choose whether to use a comma separator or not here by checking the box that says "Use 1000 Separator".

Percent Formatting

To format numbers as a percentage, highlight the cell(s), and click on the percent sign in the Number section of the Home tab or in the top row of the mini formatting menu.

This one will take the number 5 and turn it into 500% or the number 0.1 and turn it into 10%, for example, so be sure your numbers are formatted to work as percentages.

You can also highlight the cell(s), right-click, select Format Cells from the dropdown, go to the Number tab, of the Format Cells dialogue box choose Percentage on the left-hand side, and then in the middle, choose your number of decimal places.

Row Height (Adjusting)

If your rows aren't the correct height, you have three options for adjusting them.

First, you can right-click on the row you want to adjust, choose Row Height from the dropdown menu, and when the box showing you the current row height appears, enter a new row height.

Second, you can place your cursor along the lower border of the row number until it looks like a line with arrows above and below. Left-click and hold while you move the cursor up or down until the row is as tall as you want it to be.

Third, you can place your cursor along the lower border of the row, and double left-click. This will fit the row height to the text in the cell. (Usually.)

To adjust all row heights in your document at once you can highlight the entire worksheet and then double-left click on any row border and it will adjust each row to the contents in each individual row. (Again, usually. It doesn't work particularly well for cells with lots and lots of text in them.)

To have uniform row heights throughout your worksheet, you can highlight the whole sheet, right-click on a row, choose Row Height and set your row height that way or select the entire worksheet, left-click on the border below a row, and adjust that row to the height you want for all rows.

As mentioned above, to select all rows at once you can use Ctrl + A or you can click in the corner at the intersection of the rows and columns.

Underlining Text

You have three options for underlining text.

First, you can highlight your selection and type Ctrl and U at the same time. (Ctrl + U). This is the easiest method and the one I use most often.

Second, you can highlight your selection and click on the underlined U in the Font section on the Home tab. (See the Bolding section for a screen shot.)

Third, you can highlight the selection, right-click, choose Format Cells from the dropdown menu, go to the Font tab of the Format Cells dialogue box, and choose the type of underlining you want (single, double, single accounting, double accounting) from the Underline drop down menu.

As noted above, you can apply formatting to just part of the text in a cell by clicking into the cell, highlighting the portion of the text that you want to underline, and then applying your chosen format.

To remove underlining from text or cells that already have it, highlight the text or cells and then use one of the above options.

Wrapping Text

Sometimes you want to read all of the text in a cell, but you don't want that column to be wide enough to display all of the text in a single row. This is where the Wrap Text option becomes useful, because it will keep your text within the width of the column and display it on multiple lines by "wrapping" the text.

To Wrap Text in a cell, select the cell(s), go to the Alignment section of the Home Tab, and click on the Wrap Text option on the right-hand side in the Alignment section.

Or you can highlight the cell(s), right-click, choose Format Cells from the dropdown menu, go to the Alignment tab in the Format Cells dialogue box, and choose Wrap Text under the second section, Text Control.

You will likely have to adjust the row height after you do this to see all of the text. The double-click method to auto-adjust your row height will generally work here, but if you have lots of text Excel has a limit to how much it will auto-adjust the height of a row and you may have to click and drag to get the row height you need.

* * *

One final trick that I use often, probably more in Word than in Excel, but that's still handy to know:

Format Painter
(Or How To Copy Formatting From One Cell To Another)

In addition to the specific formatting options discussed above, if you already have a cell formatted the way you want it to, you can take the formatting from that cell to other cells you want formatted the same way.

You do this by using the Format Painter

First, highlight the cell(s) that have the formatting you want to copy. (If the formatting is identical across all cells then just highlight one cell.)

Next, click on the Format Painter which is either located in the bottom right corner of the mini formatting menu or in the Clipboard section of the Home tab. It looks like a little paint brush. (I call it format sweeping because it always looked like a little broom to me, but given the name it's obviously a paint brush.)

Finally, select the range of cells where you want to copy the formatting.

The contents of the destination cells will remain the same, but the font, font color, font size, cell borders, italics/bolding/underlining, text alignment and text orientation will all change to match that of the cell that you took the formatting from.

As I alluded to above, you can select a range of cells and take their formatting and apply it to another range of cells. So I can have the first cell be bold, the second be italic, the third be red, etc. and I can select that cell range and then use Format Painter to apply that same different formatting across as many cells as I swept the formatting from.

If you do that, you can just click into the first cell of the range where you're applying the formatting. Excel will change the formatting of X number of cells where X is the original range of cells you chose your formatting from.

You need to be careful using the Format Painter because it will change *all* formatting in your destination cells.

So, if the cell you're copying the formatting from is bolded and has red text, both of those attributes will copy over even if all you were trying to do was copy the bold formatting. This is more of a problem when using the tool in Word than in Excel, but it's still something to watch out for especially if you have borders around cells. If you, for example, copy formatting from a cell that's in the center of a formatted table to a cell that's on the edge of that table you could end up removing the edge border.

(If that sounds confusing, just play around with it a bit and you'll see what I'm talking about.)

Also, the tool copies formatting to whatever cell you select next, which can be a problem if the cell you're copying from isn't near the one you're copying to. I sometimes have the temptation to use the arrow keys to move to the cell where I want to place the formatting, but that obviously does not work because the minute I arrow over one cell the formatting transfers to that cell.

To avoid this issue, click directly into the cell where you want to transfer the formatting.

(And remember, that Ctrl + Z is your friend if you make a mistake.)

Also, if you have more than one isolated cell that you need to apply formatting to, you can double-click the Format Painter instead of single clicking and it will continue to copy the formatting of the original cell to every cell you click in until you click on the Format Painter again or hit Esc. (You'll know the tool is still in operation because there will be a little brush next to your cursor as you move it around.)

If you format sweep, realize you made a mistake, and then use Ctrl + Z to undo, you'll see that the cell(s) you were trying to take formatting from will be surrounded by a dotted border as if you had copied it. Hit the Esc key before you continue. Otherwise you risk copying the contents of that cell or cells to a new one if you click in another cell and hit Enter.

(Not a common problem, but one to be aware of.)

Manipulating Your Data

Once you've entered your data into a worksheet, you are then ready to work with that data by filtering it, sorting it, and performing calculations on it.

This section will walk you through the basics of selecting, sorting, filtering, and analyzing your data. I'm just going to touch on formulas and the most essential functions, but this series does have an entire book (*Excel 2019 Formulas and Functions*) that is devoted to the topic if you find that you need or want to know more. Also, PivotTables and charts can be very useful for data analysis, but those are covered in *Excel 2019 Intermediate* because the goal in this book is to firmly ground you in the basics.

So, let's start with a few quick tricks for selecting your data that you want to analyze.

Select All

I mentioned this already in the formatting chapter when we discussed changing row height and column width, but I want to cover it again. If you want to select every single active cell in a worksheet, you can use Ctrl + A. (To select all of the rows and columns in a worksheet you may need to apply it more than once because it may just select your cells with data in them the first time.)

As mentioned above, it can be helpful when trying to adjust the row height or the column width in an entire worksheet quickly.

I also use it to copy the entire contents of a worksheet at once.

I will often combine Select All with Paste Special – Values onto the same worksheet. This is a simple way to remove any formulas from the worksheet as well as any PivotTables.

Another way to select all of the cells in your worksheet is to click in the small box at the intersection of the rows and columns labels. It does the exact same thing as Ctrl + A.

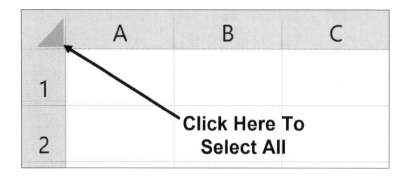

One caution when selecting all is that you don't then do something like apply borders to the entire worksheet. This can mess with your file size as well as printing because Excel stores that information for all of those cells even if you don't have any information in them. So don't do that. If you do so accidentally, you can Undo or select all and then go to the Clear dropdown in the Editing section of the Home tab and choose Clear Formats.

Select A Row

I often will want to select a row of data in my worksheet To do so, click on the row number on the left-hand side. (You may have to do it twice to select the row)

All of the cells in that row except the first one should turn gray to show that they've been selected.

Be careful about applying formatting if you do this, because you will rarely need to format an entire row and doing so can mess with printing.

To select more than one row, you can select left-click on the first row you want and then hold that down as you drag the mouse up or down to select more rows.

If the rows you need are not touching, use the Ctrl key as you click on each row number. You can also click on one row, hold down the shift key and click at the end of the range you select to select all of the rows in between.

Select A Column

Selecting a column works just like selecting a row. Click on the letter of the column you want to select. (You may have to do so twice to actually select the cells)

When the column is selected all cells in that column will be shaded gray except for the first one. You can select multiple columns by clicking and dragging, using the control key as you click on each one you want, or using the shift key to select a range of columns.

Again, selecting columns is useful for copying the data in a column or when writing a formula that references the values in a column, but don't apply formatting to the entire column.

Select A Range of Cells

It's very easy to select an entire table of data as long as it has a header row that labels all of the columns and an identifier column that has a value in it for every row of the table. (This helps define the range of columns and rows in the table.)

To do so, click in the top left corner of your data and then while holding down the Shift and Ctrl keys use the down arrow key followed by the right arrow key to highlight all of your cells in the table. (You can also arrow right and then down.)

Once the cells are selected, you can then apply all the formatting you want to that range of cells or copy it, etc.

What is happening when you do this is that you are telling Excel to start where you are and go in the direction of the arrow you used and select all of the cells it finds that have content in them until it reaches one that doesn't and then stop.

Because we were talking about a table that had column labels and row labels that selects the entire range of the table, even the blank cells within the table.

Sometimes your data won't be that neatly arranged and there will be gaps. If that happens, just keep arrowing in the direction you wanted until you reach the end of your data.

Also, I tell you to start in the top left corner of your data because that's the easiest way to make sure you select it all, but you can do this from any point. The only problem is you can go left OR right but not left AND right. Same with up and down. You can go up OR down but not up AND down. So start in a corner.

Being able to select a data range is very helpful when it comes to sorting and filtering. I can usually get away with just selecting all, but there are times when it is better to select a specific range of cells.

Also, selecting a range of cells comes in very useful when you don't want to bring over header information from another worksheet but just want the data.

Reach The End Of A Data Range

What if you want to reach the end of your data but you don't want to select it?

You can do so with just the Ctrl key and the arrows. Using Ctrl and an arrow will take you to the cell in that direction that is the last cell with something in it before an empty cell.

Depending on how your data is set up, that may not be the absolute end. But if your data is set up cleanly where it's all labeled and kept together Ctrl + an arrow key should take you to the edge of your existing data. You can then use the arrow key one more time from there to get to an empty cell.

Sorting

Now that we know how to select a range of data, let's talk about sorting.

Sorting allows you to take a data set and display it in a specific order. For example, chronologically by date, in increasing or decreasing value, or alphabetically.

Excel also allows you to sort at more than one level at a time. So you can sort by date and then by customer name and then by transaction value, for example. This would put all April 12th orders together and then all orders by each customer together, making them easy to locate.

Okay, so how do you do this?

First, select all cells that contain your information, including your header row if there is one.

(If you set your data up with the first row as the header and all of the rest as data, you can use Ctrl + A or click in the top left corner to select all.)

If you have a table of data that starts lower down on the page or that has a summary row or that is followed by other data that you don't want to use, then you need to be careful to only select the cells you want to work with.

Be very careful also to keep your data together. What I mean by that is, say you want to sort by date and customer name, but you have ten other columns of data related to each transaction by each customer on each day. You need to select all twelve columns of data even though you're only sorting on two of those columns.

If you don't do that then Excel will sort the two columns you selected but leave the other ten columns in their original position. That will mean that Customer Jones's July 3rd transaction information is now listed as Customer Smith's August 5th transaction.

So always, always before you sort make sure that all of your related data has been selected.

Once you've selected your data, go to the Editing section of the Home tab. Click on the arrow for Sort & Filter and then choose Custom Sort.

Your other option is to go to the Data tab and click on the Sort option there.

You can also right-click and choose Sort and then Custom Sort from the dropdown menu. All three options will open the Sort dialogue box.

The first choice you need to make is to indicate whether or not your data has headers. In other words, does the first row of your data contain column labels?

If so, click on that box in the top corner that says, "My data has headers." If you indicate that there is a header row, it will not be included in your sort and will remain the first row of your data.

When you do this, you'll see that your Sort By dropdown now displays your column labels.

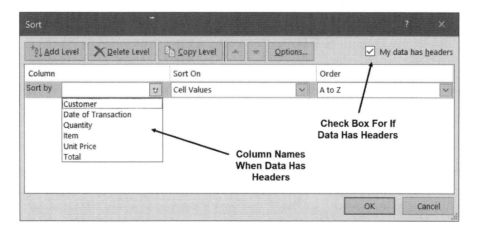

If you don't check this box, the dropdown will show generic column names (Column A, Column B, etc.) and *all* of your data will be sorted, *including* the first row.

Sometimes Excel tries to decide on its own whether there are headers or not and is wrong, so always make sure that your Sort By choices make sense given the data you selected, and that you check or uncheck the "My data has headers" box to get the result you want.

The next step is to choose your sort order.

What is the first criteria you want to sort by? In the examples I've mentioned above it would be date because I want all of my data grouped by date first and then I'll sort by customer name. But if you cared more about looking up information by customer name first and then by date of transaction you'd want to choose customer name for your first Sort By option.

Whatever that primary criteria is, choose that column from the Sort By dropdown menu.

Next, choose how to sort that column of data. You can sort on cell values, cell color, font color, or conditional formatting icon.

I almost always use values but if you were working with a data set where you'd used conditional formatting (which is discussed in detail in *Excel 2019 Intermediate*) you could, for example, sort by font color and have all of your overdue payments listed first.

After you choose what to sort on, then you can choose what order to use for your sort.

For text it's usually going to be A to Z to sort alphabetically but you can also choose Z to A to sort in reverse alphabetical order.

The third option, Custom List, is very useful for when you have text entries that should be in a specific order but that order is not alphabetical. I use this for when I have data broken down by month. I can choose Custom List and then in the Custom Lists dialogue box there are two month-based sort options. (As well as two day-of-the-week-based sort options.)

The Custom Lists dialogue box also allows you to create a brand new sort order with the NEW LIST option.

For date fields, your sort choices are Oldest to Newest, Newest to Oldest, and Custom List.

For numbers your short choices are Smallest to Largest, Largest to Smallest, and Custom List.

That's the first sort order and often it will be all you need. For example, if you just want your data sorted by month. If that's the case, click OK in the bottom right corner of the Sort dialogue box.

If, however, you want to use a second sort criteria, so sort first by date and then by customer, you need to add another level to your sort. You do this by clicking on Add Level and then repeating the same process for the next row of choosing your Column, Sort On criteria, and Order.

If you ever add a level you don't need, highlight it by clicking on the words "sort by" or "then by" on the left-hand side of the row, and then choose Delete Level from the list of options at the top of the dialogue box.

If you have listed out multiple levels to sort by but then decide that they should be sorted in a different order, you can select one of the levels and use the arrows at the top of the dialogue box to move that level up or down.

The default is to sort your data from top to bottom, so in rows.

Row 2 (assuming you have a header in Row 1) will be the first entry based on your sort criteria, Row 3 will be the second, etc.

You can click on Options in the Sort dialogue box, however, if you want to sort across columns instead.

(I think I've only ever needed to do that once. But just spitballing here, if I had, for example, a table of information and had listed student names across my columns and wanted those sorted alphabetically so that Column B was Anna and Column C was Bob, etc. I could use this option to make that happen.)

Options is also where you can do a case-sensitive sort, but I've never found myself needing to do that.

When you're done with all of your sort options, click OK.

(If you change your mind about performing a sort, click Cancel.)

Immediately check your results. Look across an entire row of data and ask if that still makes sense. Did you properly select and sort the data so that all of Customer Smith's transaction information stayed together?

If not, use Ctrl + Z to undo and try again because if you save the file with a bad sort order it's done for. You'll have to go back to your original raw data and start over. (Assuming you were smart enough to save your raw data in one location and do any analysis work in another. Which you should always, always do. As discussed previously and in *Data Principles for Beginners*.)

One final note about sorting, Excel also offers quick-sort options (the ones that say Sort A to Z or Sort Z to A) which are basically options to sort in ascending or descending order based upon the cell you're in at the time you make the selection.

Theoretically these options identify your data range, figure out if you have a header or not, and then sort based on the column you chose. But be wary when using them. Sometimes they work great, most times they sort in the wrong order for me or on the wrong column or miss that I have a header row.

Filtering

Okay. Now on to filtering which is also incredibly useful. I often won't need to permanently change the order of my data, I just want to see a subset of my data that meets a certain criteria. For example, I only want to see sales for Title A or Author B.

Filtering allows me to do that without having to sort.

This works best with a data table that has continuous and labeled columns and continuous rows.

If you have non-continuous columns, you need to manually select all of your columns when you choose to filter in order for the filter option to show for all of them. Otherwise, Excel will only show the filter option for the column in which you were clicked at the time you turned on filtering as well as for any columns that are connected to that column.

This sounds confusing, so let me show you what I mean.

	A	B	C	D	E	F	G
1	Customer	Date of Transaction		Quantity	Item	Unit Price	Total
2	Richard Martinez	4/7/2016		20	Whasit	$ 1.50	$ 30.00
3	Richard Martinez	3/7/2016		10	Who knows what	$ 3.50	$ 35.00
4	Albert Jones	9/1/2015		3	Whatchamacallit	$ 15.00	$ 45.00
5	Albert Jones	8/30/2015		10	Widget	$ 25.00	$250.00
6	Albert Jones	8/1/2015		1	Widget	$ 20.00	$ 20.00
7	Albert Jones	8/1/2015		1	Other	$ 5.00	$ 5.00
8							

Here I have six columns of data, but I have a blank column in Column C so that the data is not continuous. When I click into Cell A1 and turn on filtering, it only turns on filtering for Columns A and B. (You can tell filtering is on by looking at those little arrows in the corners in Cells A1 and B1.)

Because Column C was blank, Excel didn't know to also turn on filtering for Columns D, E, F, and G. I can work around this by turning off filtering, selecting Cells A1 through G1 and turning filtering back on. That will apply filtering to all of the columns.

Or I can make my life simpler and simply not have the blank column in the middle of my data in which case when I click into Cell A1 (or any of the cells in Row 1) filtering will be available for all of the columns of data.

If for some reason you don't want to filter starting at the top row of your data, you can highlight a row of data that is not at the top of the range and Excel will apply the filtering options starting at the highlighted row. (Usually for me what happens is I do that accidentally and notice that the filtering is in Row 3 where my data is instead of Row 1 where my header row is and I have to go turn off filtering and reapply it at Row 1.)

To apply filtering, click into the appropriate spot in your data, and then in the Editing section of the Home tab, click on the arrow next to Sort & Filter and choose Filter.

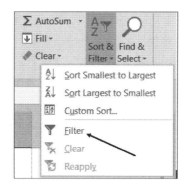

Once you turn on filtering you should see small gray arrows in the bottom right corner of each cell in your header row. (Like on the previous page with Customer and Date of Transaction in Cells A1 and B1.)

Filtering in Excel has evolved over the years, which means the complex type of filtering we're about to discuss was not always available in prior versions of Excel. So if you filter a file and try to share that with someone using an older version of Excel it may do weird things. Namely, they won't be able to remove or adjust your filtering easily. (Easy way to deal with that is never save your data in a filtered form.)

Okay, so let's talk filtering options. Once you have filtering turned on, you can click on that little arrow in the corner at the top of a column and it will bring up a dropdown menu that has a variety of options for you to use to filter the contents of your data table. (See the next page for an example.)

The very top options in that dropdown are sort options.

The first filter option, Filter by Color, will generally be grayed out unless you have different font colors or fill colors in your data.

If you have used different font or fill colors, you can hold your cursor over where it says Filter by Color and it will then give you additional options to Filter by Cell Color or Filter by Font Color.

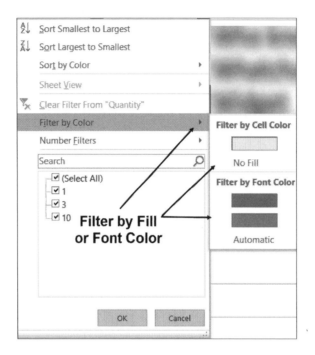

These options will only show the font or fill colors you've used in your data. If you want cells that are the standard color or the standard fill you can choose the No Fill or the Automatic filtering choices.

After the filter by color choices, there is another set of filter options that will be named based upon the type of data in that column. Above you can see that the next option is Number Filters, but you may also see Date Filters or Text Filters.

Holding your cursor over this option will show filter criteria for that type of data. For numbers you'll see choices such as Equals, Greater Than, Between, etc. For dates you'll see Before, After, Tomorrow, Today, etc. For text you'll see Begins With, Contains, etc.

I find these options to be useful when there are a large number of individual entries that all differ slightly from one another but that I want to include in my display. So if I want all of my Excel books, for example, I can use a Contains filter and look for entries with "Excel" in them. That's much easier than going through and checking boxes to select each title individually.

The filter approach I probably use the most, though, is the final option which is the checkbox option. You can see above and on the next page that the dropdown will list the possible values for that column with checkboxes next to each value. You can select one or more of the values in that list by checking or unchecking the box next to each value.

If you just want one value and there are a number of choices, click in that Select All box at the top to unselect everything and then go back and click on the entries you want. It's much faster than unchecking everything one box at a time.

You also have the option to use the Search field that's directly above the checkboxes. Excel will filter your data down to just those entries that contain the search term and then you can refine from there if you need to.

When cells in your worksheet are filtered, the row numbers in your worksheet will be colored blue, and you'll see that the row numbers skip since some rows won't be displayed. (In the screenshot below, Row 2 is not displayed because it had a date in April 2016 and I unchecked that box.)

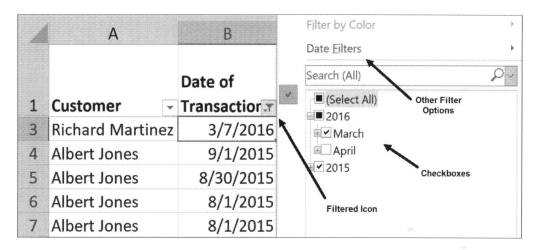

Columns where filtering is in place will show a funnel instead of an arrow on the gray dropdown next to the column name.

To remove filtering from a specific column, click on the gray arrow, and select Clear Filter from [Column Name] in the dropdown menu.

To remove all filtering you've applied to a worksheet, go to the Editing section of the Home tab, click on Sort & Filter, and then choose Clear. This will leave the filtering option in place but remove all filters.

To remove filtering altogether, go to the Editing section of the Home tab, click on Sort & Filter, and click on Filter.

Some of this can also be done through right-click and using the dropdown available on the worksheet. If you're clicked into a cell and want to filter by that value or fill color or font color, you can right-click, move your cursor to the Filter option, and then choose Filter by Selected Cell's Value, Color, Font Color, or Icon. That will perform the filter task you wanted as well as turning on filtering for that range of cells.

Once filtering is on, you can also right-click, go to Filter, and choose to clear the filter from a specific column.

Because the right-click option is somewhat limited, I tend to just use the Editing section of the Home tab.

* * *

Basic Math Calculations

Alright, that was sorting and filtering. Now let's talk basic math calculations in Excel. I'm going to cover addition, subtraction, multiplication, and division.

Let's start with doing each of those tasks using standard math notation.

In Excel these are referred to as calculation operators, but you'll probably recognize them as the way you used to write an equation in math class.

For addition, you use a plus sign (+). For subtraction, you use a minus sign (-). For multiplication you use an asterisk (*). For division, you use a forward slash (/).

To perform one of these basic calculations in a cell in Excel, click into the cell where you want to perform the calculation, type an equals sign, type the first value you want to use, type the calculation operator for the calculation you want to perform (+ - * /), and then type the second value you want to use. Hit Enter. You will see the result of that calculation in the cell and if you go back to the cell you'll see your equation in the formula bar.

So, for example:

=23+23

would add 23 and 23 and when you hit enter you would see a value of 46 in that cell.

=23/23

would divide 23 by 23 and you would see a value of 1 in that cell after you hit enter.

=4*5

would return a value of 20.

And

$$=10\text{-}2$$

would return a value of 8.

If that's all that Excel could do it wouldn't be very useful. About as useful as a calculator. The power that Excel has is that it can perform those same calculations by using cell references. So rather than type in 23, you can have the value 23 in a cell and point Excel at that cell to retrieve the value for you.

That still doesn't sound too exciting until you realize that you can combine that task with copying formulas which means you can write a simple formula that says add this cell in Column A to that cell in Column B and then copy that one formula you wrote a hundred thousand times with a single click, and have Excel add those two cells in those two columns for all hundred thousand rows of your data in less than a minute.

But to make that happen requires using cell notation instead of numbers.

The easy way to use cell notation is to let Excel do it for you by simply clicking on the cells you want as you build your formula.

So you click in the cell where you want your calculation, type an equals sign, click on the cell that contains the first value you want to use in your calculation, type your calculation operator (+ - * /), and then click on the cell that contains the second value you want to use in your calculation, and then hit enter.

Excel will build your formula for you and write the name of the cell you click on each time into your formula.

You can even see if the correct cells were used by going back to the cell where you did the calculation and double-clicking on it. Excel will show you the formula it wrote and highlight all of the cells it used in the formula as well as color code each cell and cell reference in the formula. Cell A2 will be blue and the text A2 in the formula will also be blue, for example, so you can see exactly where each value was used.

Which is great, but I like to understand how to do it myself so I can better troubleshoot issues. So let's cover how that works real quick.

First, a quick refresher about how you reference a cell. A cell is the intersection of a row and a column and is always written with the column identifier first. So if I write A1 that means the cell that's at the intersection of Column A and Row 1. (You don't have to include Cell when you write this in a formula because that's implied.) Likewise, B2 is the cell that is at the intersection of Column B and Row 2.

To reference more than one cell at a time, you need to use either a colon (:) or a comma (,).

A comma (,) written between two cell references means "and.". So

A1,B3

means Cells A1 and B3.

A colon (:) written between two cell references means "through". So

A1:B3

means all cells in Columns A and B and all cells in those columns that are in Rows 1, 2, and 3.

Likewise,

D24:M65

means all cells in Columns D through M and in Rows 24 through 65.

To reference an entire column, you just leave out the row numbers. So

B:B

means all of the cells in Column B. And

B:C

means all of the cells in Columns B and C.

To reference an entire row you leave out the column letters. So

2:2

means all of the cells in Row 2. And

2:10

means all of the cells in Rows 2 through 10.

Putting that together with what we discussed earlier about using calculation operators, the following are how you would write addition, subtraction, multiplication, and division of values in Cells A1 and B1:

=A1+B1

$$=A1-B1$$

$$=A1*B1$$

$$=A1/B1$$

Remember from math class that with addition and multiplication order isn't going to matter, A1+B1 and B1+A1 give you the same result. But with subtraction and division, which value is listed first will impact the result you get. A1-B1 and B1-A1 are different equations.

Which is why there is no shortcut, quickie way to subtract or divide multiple values in Excel. But for addition and multiplication there are. You can use what are called functions to sum or multiply any number of cells that you want.

The function you use for addition is SUM. The function you use for multiplication is PRODUCT. (I often use SUM, I rarely use PRODUCT although I do use one we won't cover here that is SUMPRODUCT that combines the two.)

If you're going to use a function for a calculation, you click into the cell, type your equals sign, then type the function you want and an opening paren, then you type your cell references or highlight the cells you want, then type a closing paren and hit enter.

This table shows how to use the operators when just using two values and how to use the functions or operators when dealing with multiple values:

	With Two Values In Cells A1 and B1	With Six Values In Cells A1, B1, A2, B2, A3, and B3
Addition	=A1+B1	=SUM(A1:B3)
Subtraction	=A1-B1	=A1-B1-A2-B2-A3-B3
Multiplication	=A1*B1	=PRODUCT(A1:B3)
Division	=A1/B1	=A1/B1/A2/B2/A3/B3

A few more comments:

With addition, there are two other tricks to know.

First, if you don't care about recording the value you calculate, you can simply highlight the cells you want to add together and then look in the bottom right corner of the worksheet. It should show you the average, the count, and the sum of the cells you have highlighted.

Second you can use the AutoSum option in the Editing section of the Home Tab to add either a row or column of values without having to type in the formula. This is basically just another way to have Excel create your formula for you.

To use it, click into the empty cell at the end of your range of values and then click on the AutoSum icon which looks like the mathematical sum function (a big pointy E-like shape). Excel will then create and display a SUM function for you and highlight the cells it thinks you wanted to add.

The AutoSum option stops at blank cells, so if you need to sum across a blank space, you'll need to edit the formula for it to work properly, but it can be a nice way to get a quick start on writing your formula.

(You'll note that there's a dropdown there as well, so you can also use it for Average, Count Numbers, Max, and Min.)

Complex Formulas

Excel can handle incredibly complex formulas. You just have to make sure you write them properly so that Excel knows which functions to perform first.

Put something in parens and Excel will do that before anything else. Otherwise it will follow standard mathematical principles about which actions to perform in which order.

According to the Excel help documentation (under Operator Precedence), Excel will first combine cells (B1:B3 or B1,B2), then create any negative numbers (-B1). Next it will create percents, then calculate any exponentials (B2^2), then do any multiplication and division, then do any addition and subtraction, then concatenate any values, and then do any comparisons last.

All of this, of course, at least in the U.S., is done from left to right in a formula.

So, basically, Excel calculates starting on the left side of the equation and moves to the right, doing each of those steps above in that order throughout the entire formula before circling back to the start and doing the next step. Which means that multiplication and division are done first and then addition or subtraction.

Of course, anything in parens is treated as a standalone equation first. So if you have =3*(4+2), Excel will add the 4 and the 2 before it does the multiplication.

Basically, if you're going to write complex formulas they're definitely doable but you should be very comfortable with math and how it works. Also, be sure to test your equation to make sure you did it right. I do this by breaking a formula into its component steps and then making sure that my combined equation generates the same result.

Other Functions

We briefly discussed SUM and PRODUCT, but Excel has hundreds of available functions that can do all sorts of interesting things and not just with numbers.

To see what I'm talking about, go to the Formulas tab. There are seven different subject areas listed there (Financial, Logical, Text, Date & Time, Lookup & Reference, Math & Trig, and More Functions which shows an additional six categories). Click on each of those dropdowns and you'll see twenty-plus functions for each one.

But how do you know if there's a function that does what you want to do? For example, is there a function for trimming excess space from a string of values? (Yes. It's called TRIM.) Or for calculating the cumulative principal paid on a loan between two periods? (Yes.)

So how do you find the function you want without hovering over each function to see what it does because the names by themselves are certainly no help?

The simple way is to go to the Formulas tab and click on Insert Function. This will bring up the Insert Function dialogue box which includes a search function. Type a few words for what you're looking for.

For example, if I want to calculate how many days until some event occurs and I want to have this formula work no matter what day it is when I open my worksheet, then I need some way to set a value equal to today's date whatever day today is. So I search for "today" and get a function called TODAY that it says "Returns the current date formatted as a date." Perfect.

Once you've found a function you like, select it and click on OK. Excel will take you back to the worksheet and show you a Function Arguments dialogue box that tells you what inputs are needed to create that particular function.

If the function doesn't require any arguments, like TODAY doesn't, it will just let you know that and insert the function into your selected cell.

Sometimes selecting a function this way, even if you know what it does, is helpful because it shows you what order you need to put the information in and what form it needs to take. But you can also see this to a lesser degree when you start to type the function into your cell. Once you type the opening paren it will show you the components you need and their order. (Very helpful for things like SUMIF and SUMIFS that have different orders even though they do similar things.)

As mentioned before, *Excel 2019 Formulas and Functions*, which is 200 pages long, is going to be the best resource if you really want to dig in on how formulas and functions work.

Copying Cells With Formulas in Them

One of the nice things about working with formulas in Excel is that you don't have to type them over and over and over again. You can type a formula once and if you need to use it again, simply copy it to a new cell.

There are some tricks to copying formulas. So let's walk through those.

By default, formulas are relative. Meaning that if you have a formula that says

$$=B1+C1$$

and you copy it (Ctrl + C) over to the right one cell it will become

$$=C1+D1$$

See how the column value for each referenced cell changed by one column? If you copy that same formula down one cell from the original location it will become

$$=B2+C2$$

See how the row number for each referenced cell changed by one?

This is great when you have rows and rows of data with everything located in the same position and want to perform the exact same calculation on each of those rows. You can simply copy the formula and paste it down the entire column and it will perform that calculation on each and every row.

But sometimes you just want to move the calculation. Say it's in Cell B2 now and you want to put it in Cell A10. That's when you need to cut the formula (Ctrl + X) instead of copy it. By cutting and moving the formula, it stays the exact same. If it said =B1+C1 before it still will after you paste it into the new location..

Another way to do this is to click into the cell, highlight all of the text in the cell, copy it, and tab (or Esc) out of the cell, and then click on the new location and paste it that way.

(If you click into the cell, highlight all of the text, and try to click on where you want to paste it, you'll end up replacing your existing text in the source cell with a reference to the cell you clicked into.)

What if you want to copy the formula, but you want to keep some portion of it fixed? Say either the row reference, the column reference, or the reference to an entire cell. (Useful when calculating different scenarios where you build a table with different values for variable x in one row and different values for variable y in one column and then calculate what value you get for each combination of x and y. So, hourly pay and hours worked, for example.)

You can fix a portion of a cell reference by using the $ sign. (We discussed it earlier with respect to inputting data, but I'll run through it again here.)

To fix the reference to a cell, put a $ sign before both the letter and the number in the cell name. So cell B2 becomes B2 in your formula.

If you reference a cell that way (B2), no matter where you copy that formula to it will continue to reference that specific cell.

This is useful if you have a constant value in your formula. So say you're selling widgets and they're all priced at $100. You might list Widget Price at the top of your worksheet and put 100 in a cell at the top and then calculate how much each customer owes by multiplying their units purchased by that fixed value in that cell.

If you want to keep just the column the same, but change the row reference, then put the dollar sign in front of the letter only. So $B2 when copied would become $B3, $B4, etc. no matter where you copy that formula to it's always B.

If you want to keep the row the same, but change the column reference, you'd put the dollar sign in front of the number only. So B$2. When copied, that portion of the formula would change to C$2, D$2, etc. but the 2 would never change.

One more thought about copying formulas. I usually just highlight all of the cells where I want to copy the formula to and then paste, but there's a shortcut that you can sometimes use that's faster when you have many many rows of data.

If you have a formula in a cell and want to copy it downward and the column where that cell is located is touching another column of data that has already been completed (so you have a full column of data next to the column where you want to put your formula), you can place your cursor on the bottom right corner of the cell with the formula and double-left click. This should copy the formula down all of your rows of data.

It doesn't work if the other column of data hasn't been filled in yet. Excel only knows how far to copy the formula based on the information in the other column. But it can be a handy shortcut in a table with lots of completed information where you're just adding a calculation.

Okay. So that was manipulating data, let's now talk about how to print when you have a finished product that's ready to go.

Printing

You might not think that printing needs its own section, but it definitely does. Not because clicking on Print is so hard to do, but because you need to format your data well to get it to print well. If you just hit print without thinking about how that information in your worksheet will appear on a printed page, you'll likely end up with pages and pages worth of poorly-formatted garbage.

Now, it's possible you have no intent of printing anything (I never print my budget spreadsheet) in which case, skip this section. But if you are going to print, let's try and waste as little paper as possible.

First things first. To print, go to the File tab and select Print.

Typing Ctrl and P at the same time (Ctrl + P) will also take you to the print screen.

You should see a number of print options in the center of the screen and a preview section on the right-hand side.

If everything looks good, you can just click on the big Print button right there at the top and be done with it.

Sometimes that's the case if you're printing a small amount of data, but usually I find I need to make adjustments, especially if I have enough information that it carries over to additional pages.

Let's walk through all of the options you have with respect to printing, but first let me just show you what the print screen will look like:

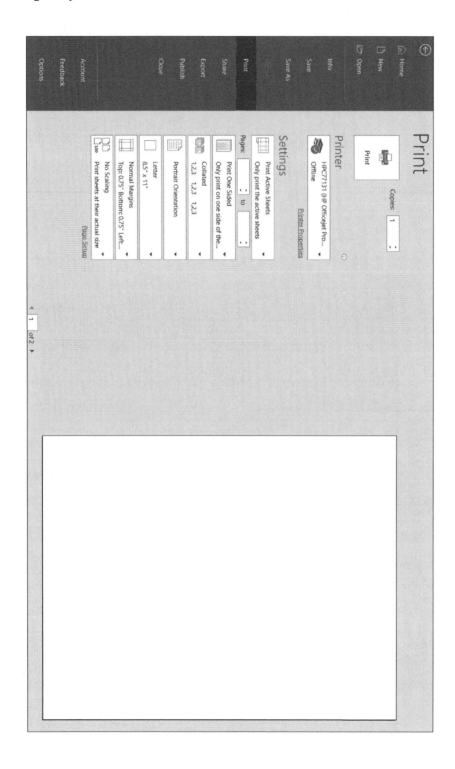

You can see in the image that you have a number of print options listed underneath the text Print and then on the right-hand side you have a print preview of what your document will look like on a page-by-page basis.

(In this case, mine is blank but you can see at the bottom where it says 1 of 2 and you can arrow to a second page.)

Let's walk through each of those options starting with the image of a printer right under the text Print.

Print

Once you're ready to print your page, you can click on the button on the top left with the image of a printer that says Print and your document will print.

Copies

To the right of that image where it says Copies is where you specify how many copies to print. If you want to print more than one copy, change that number by either using the up and down arrows or by clicking into the box and typing in a new value.

Printer

It should display your computer's default printer here, but if you want to use a different printer than that one, click on the arrow next to the printer name and choose from the listed options. If the printer you want isn't listed, choose Add Printer.

Print Active Sheets / Print Entire Workbook / Print Selection

The default is Print Active Sheets. This will generally be the worksheet you were working in when you chose to print.

However, you can select more than one worksheet by holding down the Control key and clicking on multiple worksheet names. (When you do this, you'll see that the names of all of your selected worksheets are highlighted, not just one of them.) If you do this before you choose to print, then when you do Print Active Sheets it will print all of the worksheets you've selected.

I would only print multiple worksheets if you're satisfied that each one is formatted exactly the way you want it formatted.

Also, choosing to print more than one sheet at a time either with Print Active Sheets or Print Entire Workbook, results in strange things happening to your headers and footers. For example, your pages will be numbered across worksheets. If you mean each worksheet to be a standalone report with numbered pages specific to that report, then you need to print each worksheet separately.

As I just alluded to, the Print Entire Workbook option prints all of the worksheets in your workbook. Print Selection allows you to just print a highlighted section of a worksheet or worksheets.

(I happened to have three worksheets selected at once and then highlighted the first twenty cells in one of those worksheets and when I went to Print Selection Excel printed those twenty cells in *each* of those three worksheets.)

Pages

Just below the Print Active Sheets option is a row that says Pages and has two boxes with arrows at the side. You can choose to just print a specific page rather than the entire worksheet by using the options here. To figure out which page to print, look at your preview. To specify the pages numbers either use the up and down arrows or click into the boxes and type in your value(s) using commas between page numbers.

Print One Sided / Print on Both Sides (long edge) / Print on Both Sides (short edge)

The default is to just print on one side of your paper. If you have a printer that can print on both sides of the page you can change your settings to do so. You want the long-edge option if your layout is going to be portrait-style and the short-edge option if your layout is going to be landscape-style. (See below.)

Whether or not you have the option to choose to print on both sides will depend on the printer you have selected. I have occasionally printed to PDF and then come back to print in Excel and found that I couldn't print on both sides because my printer had been changed to the PDF option and I had forgotten to change it back.

Collated / Uncollated

This only matters if what you're printing has more than one page and if you're printing more than one copy.

In that case, you need to decide if you want to print one full copy at a time x number of times or if you want to print x copies of page 1 and then x copies of page 2 and then x copies of page 3 and so on until you've printed all pages of your document. In general, I would choose collated (one copy at a time), which is also the default. The uncollated option (one page at a time) could be good for handouts.

Portrait Orientation / Landscape Orientation

You can choose to print in either portrait orientation (with the short edge of the page on top) or landscape orientation (with the long edge of the page on top). You can see what difference it will make by changing the option in Excel and looking at your print preview.

Which option you choose will likely depend on how many columns of data you have.

Assuming I'm dealing with a normal worksheet with rows of data listed across various columns, my goal is to fit all of my columns on one page if possible. Sometimes changing the layout to landscape allows me to do that because it allows me to have more columns per page than I'd be able to fit in portrait mode.

If I have just a few columns of data, but lots of rows I'll generally stick with portrait orientation instead.

You'll have to decide what works best for you and your specific situation.

Letter / Legal / Statement / Etc.

This is where you select your paper type. Unless you're in an office, chances are you'll leave this exactly like it is. I'm sure my printer could print on legal paper, but I don't have any for it to use so it's a moot point for me. In the U.S. the default is. 8.5"x11" but I assume that overseas it is A4 or some other regional standard.

Normal Margins / Wide Margins / Narrow Margins / Custom Margins

I would expect you won't use this often, but if you need to then this would be where you can change the margins on your document. The normal margins allow for .7" on each side and .75" on top and bottom. If you have a lot of text and need just a little more room to fit it all on one page, you could use the narrow margin option to make that happen. I generally adjust my scaling instead although that does change the text size which changing the margins will not do.

No Scaling / Fit Sheet on One Page / Fit All Columns on One Page / Fit All Rows on One Page/ Custom Scaling Options

I use this option often when I have a situation where my columns are just a little bit too much to fit on the page or my rows go just a little bit beyond the page. If you choose "Fit All Columns on One Page" that will make sure that all of your columns fit across the top of one page. You might still have multiple pages because of the number of rows, but at least everything will fit across the top.

Of course, depending on how many columns you have, this might not be a good choice. Excel will make it fit, but it does so by decreasing your font size. If you have too many columns you're trying to fit on one page your font size may become so small you can't read it.

So be sure to look at your preview before you print. (And use Landscape Orientation first if you need to.)

Fit All Rows on One Page is good for if you have maybe one or two rows too many to naturally fit on the page.

Fit Sheet on One Page is a combination of fitting all columns and all rows onto one page. Again, Excel will do it if you ask it to, but with a large set of data you won't be able to read it.

Custom Scaling brings up the Page Setup dialogue box. This is often where I will go to adjust my scaling for a document because it has the most flexibility. You can specify exactly how many pages to scale by in each direction. (We'll talk about that more below.)

Page Setup

The Page Setup link at the very bottom of the Print Screen Options gives you access to even more print options by opening the Page Setup dialogue box.

A few things to point out to you that I find useful:

1. Scaling

On the Page tab you can see the scaling option once more in the second section of the box where it says Scaling.

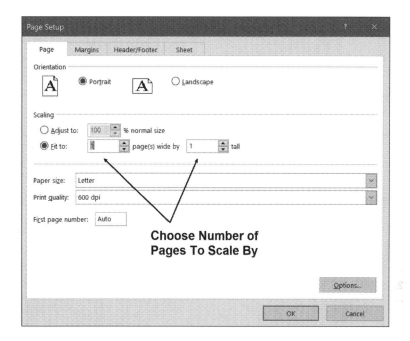

Choose Number of
Pages To Scale By

The nice thing here is that you can fit your information to however many pages across by however many pages long. You're not limited to 1 page wide or 1 page tall.

So say you have a document that's currently one page wide and four pages long but the last page is just one row. You can scale that document in the Page Setup dialogue box so that the document that prints is one page wide by three pages long and that last row is brought up onto the prior page.

2. Center Horizontally or Vertically

On the Margins tab there are two check boxes that let you center what you're printing either horizontally or vertically on the page, or both.

I will often choose to center an item horizontally if there aren't many columns.

3. Header/Footer

We're going to talk about another way to do this in a moment, but if you want to set up a header and/or a footer for your printed document you can do so on the Header/Footer tab.

The dropdown boxes that say (none) include a number of pre-formatted headers and footers for you to use. So if you just want the page number included, there should be a pre-formatted one that you can select via the dropdown options.

Same with including the worksheet name or file name in the header or footer. As you look at each one it will show you examples of the actual text that will be included. You also have the option of customizing either the header or footer.

4. Sheet

The sheet tab has a couple of useful options, but I'm going to show you a different way to set these options through the Page Layout Tab.

Page Layout Tab

If you exit out of the File tab go back to your worksheet by clicking the little arrow in the top left corner of the screen or using Esc, you'll see that one of the tabs you have available to use is called Page Layout. There are certain attributes that I set up here *before* I print my documents. (Or that I come back here to set up if I forget before I try to print, which is more often the case.)

Let's walk through them.

(Also, note that you can change margins, orientation, and size here just as easily as in the print preview screen.)

1. Print Area

If you only want to print a portion of a worksheet, you can set that portion as your print area by highlighting it and then clicking on the arrow next to Print Area and choosing Set Print Area in the Page Setup section of the Page Layout tab.

Only do it this way (as opposed to highlighting the section and choosing Print-Selection) if it's a permanent setting. Because once you set your print area it will remain set until you clear it. You can add more data to your worksheet but it will never print until you change your print area or clear that setting and it's easy to forget you've done that and then not be able to figure out why the whole document won't print for you.

I use this setting when I have a worksheet that either has extra information I don't want to print or where the formatting extends beyond my data and Excel keeps trying to print all those empty but formatted cells. (Sometimes removing that extra formatting is more of a hassle than it's worth and using print area is a quick workaround.)

2. Breaks

You can set where a page break occurs in your worksheet. So say you have a worksheet that takes up four pages and you want to make sure that rows 1 through 10 are on a page together and then rows 11 through 20 are on a page together even though that's not how things would naturally fall.

You can set a page break to force that to happen by clicking in a cell in your worksheet and then going to Breaks and choosing Insert Page Break from the dropdown menu. This will insert a page break above the cell where you clicked and to the left of the cell.

You can see where the breaks are located because Excel will insert a solid line through your worksheet above your selected cell and, if it wasn't the first column, to the left of your selected cell. It's not terribly easy to see in the worksheet itself, but if you go to print and look at the preview you'll see that your information is now broken into new pages at the place or places where you inserted the break(s).

To remove a page break, click into the cell below it or to the right of it and go to Breaks in the Page Setup section of the Page Layout tab and choose Remove Page Break. You can also choose Reset All Page Breaks.

Personally, I find page breaks a challenge to work with, so I usually try to get what I need some other way.

3. Print Titles

This is the one we came here to discuss. I find Print Titles incredibly valuable. When you click on this option you'll see that it brings up the Page Setup dialogue box and takes you to the Sheet tab. The top section of the Sheet tab lets you choose rows to repeat at the top of every page or columns to repeat at the left. This is invaluable. If you learn nothing else about printing, learn this.

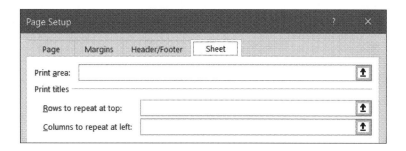

Why? Say you have a worksheet with a thousand rows of data in it that will print on a hundred pages. How do you know what's in each column on each page? You need a header row. And you need that header row to repeat at the top of each and every page.

"Rows to repeat at top" is where you specify what row(s) is your header row. Click in that box and then click on the row number in your worksheet that you want to have repeat at the top of each page. Excel will do its thing and put $1:$1 or whatever row reference it needs to for you. (You can also just type this same information in from the Print screen if you remember cell notation. Just use $ signs and your row or row numbers that you want. So $1:$3 would repeat Rows 1 through 3 on every page.)

To set a column(s) you want to repeat on the left-hand side of each page, such as a customer name or student name or record number, click in the box that says "Columns to repeat at left", and then click on the letter for the column(s) you want to repeat on each page. Again, Excel will do its magic and convert that to cell notation for you. But, again, you can write it yourself I you want, too by using $ and the letter for the column. So, $C:$C would repeat the values in Column C on every page.

Do be careful if you're going to choose more than one row or column to repeat that you don't end up selecting so many rows or columns to repeat that you basically just print the same thing over and over and over again. You need to leave room for the rest of the data in your worksheet.

Conclusion

Alright, so there you have it. A beginner's guide to Excel. This wasn't meant to be a comprehensive guide to Excel, but to instead give you the basics you need to do 95% of what you'll ever want to do in Excel. I hope it did that.

If something wasn't clear or you have any questions, please feel free to reach out to me at mlhumphreywriter@gmail.com.

As I mentioned previously, the next book in this series is *Excel 2019 Intermediate* which covers more advanced topics such as charts, pivot tables, conditional formatting, subtotaling and grouping data, and limiting the set of values that can be entered into a cell.

There is also *Excel 2019 Formulas and Functions* which gets much more in depth about how formulas and functions work in Excel and then goes one-by-one through about sixty functions in detail while covering approximately one hundred functions total.

But you can also just research specific topics on your own. The Microsoft website has a number of tutorials and examples that I think are very well-written and easy to follow at www.support.office.com. I usually find what I need there with a quick internet search for something like "bold text Excel 2019" and then choose the Microsoft support link to take me directly to the page I need.

The help available directly in Excel 2019 is excellent as well. Click on the Help tab and then click on the blue circle with a question mark that says Help. This will bring up a search box on the right-hand side of the screen where you can type in the topic that you need to know more about.

Another source of more information is to simply hold your mouse over the tasks listed on the various tabs. This will usually show a brief description of what that item does. A lot of the descriptions also have a "tell me more" link at the bottom of the description that will take you directly to the help screen related to that item. (The Format Painter on the Home tab is a good example of this. Just hold your cursor over it to see what I'm talking about.)

Your final option is to wade into the mess that is online help forums. I generally recommend against asking your own question in those forums because I find they're full of people who are rude if you don't ask your question in just the right way and provide every little piece of detailed information when you originally ask your question. How can a new user know what they don't know or what they need to provide to get their answer, right, so it always annoys me to see that.

But sometimes finding where someone else asked your question already and seeing what the answer was can be very helpful. Forums are best for the "is this possible" type of question rather than the "how does this work" type of question. Microsoft is very good at providing enough help on how things work that you can find that on their website or in the Excel help tab. But they are less helpful at telling you whether you can do something.

Again, if there's something specific you want to know, just ask. Happy to help if I can.

And thanks for reading this guide. Excel is an incredibly powerful tool and now that you have the foundation you need to use it effectively, I hope you see that.

Control Shortcuts

The following is a list of useful control shortcuts in Excel. For each one, hold down the Ctrl key and use the listed letter to perform the command.

Command	Ctrl +
Bold	B
Copy	C
Cut	X
Find	F
Italicize	I
Next Worksheet	Page Down
Paste	V
Print	P
Prior Worksheet	Page Up
Redo	Y
Replace	H
Save	S
Select All	A
Underline	U
Undo	Z

INDEX

About the Author

M.L. Humphrey is a former stockbroker with a degree in Economics from Stanford and an MBA from Wharton who has spent close to twenty years as a regulator and consultant in the financial services industry.

You can reach M.L. Humphrey at:

mlhumphreywriter@gmail.com

or at

www.mlhumphrey.com

Made in the USA
Monee, IL
14 March 2022

92855446R00061